THE WRATH OF GRAPES

Avon Books are available at special quantity discounts for bulk purchases for sales promotions, premiums, fund raising or educational use. Special books, or book excerpts, can also be created to fit specific needs.

For details write or telephone the office of the Director of Special Markets, Avon Books, Inc., Dept. FP, 1350 Avenue of the Americas, New York, New York 10019, 1-800-238-0658.

THE WRATH OF GRAPES

THE COMING WINE INDUSTRY SHAKEOUT AND HOW TO TAKE ADVANTAGE OF IT

LEWIS PERDUE

SPIKE

AN AVON BOOK

AVON BOOKS, INC.

1350 Avenue of the Americas
New York, New York 10019

Copyright © 1999 by Lewis Perdue
Published by arrangement with the author
Library of Congress Catalog Card Number: 99-94863
ISBN: 0-380-80151-5
www.spikebooks.com

First Spike Printing: June 1999

SPIKE TRADEMARK REG. U.S. PAT. OFF. AND IN OTHER COUNTRIES, MARCA
REGISTRADA, HECHO EN U.S.A.

Printed in the U.S.A.

OPM   10   9   8   7   6   5   4   3   2   1

To Mary Evelyn Arnold,
Kate's godmother and a true friend through thick and thin.

Thou hast shewed thy people hard things:
thou has made us to drink the wine of astonishment.

—PSALMS 60:3

Contents

Foreword

Whether you want to know how California's wine personalities really work, why the wine business is such a high-wire act, or how the industry is betting on the future, this book is a must (and fun) read.

Even I, a disdainer of wine literature and ill-disciplined reader in general, found part after part of this work almost physically hard to put down.

Take it from someone who grew up in the industry: if you want a clear, full, and cutting view of the business of wine, you've already opened the right book.

Enjoy!

Don Sebastiani
CEO
Sebastiani Vineyards

PART I

How to Make a Small Fortune in the Wine Business

There's a common saying in the wine business that to make a small fortune, you need to start with a large one.

It's poignant wisdom in light of the wave of bankruptcies and winery failures that shook the California wine industry in the early 1990s, taking with it family and individual fortunes both large and small. Back then, a majority of California wineries were spilling more red ink than grape juice, and as a result, more than half of the money losers were already in Chapter 11, headed for it, or looking for a buyer to avoid it.

The fact is, a similar shakeout is shaping up for the next few years. Consumption is not growing nearly fast enough to absorb a looming glut that will hammer prices downward. Bad for wineries, good for you if you wait to buy until prices have dropped.

And as with all downturns, there are ways for you to profit by investing (or resisting an investment) in both wines and wineries and their stock. But profiting in this way means being an intelligent investor, and that means knowing about the industry choke points and hot buttons: how the current fouled-up distribution system is changing, how government regulation exerts anticompetitive pressures (but maybe not for long), why there's no substantive industry marketing or research program and how that is likely to hurt wineries and the industry as a whole. Learning about each of these factors will help you handicap any wine investment.

Whether you produce it or consume it, wine is like fine art: you should spend your money on whatever produces the greatest enjoyment. In other words, whether you're in it just for the drinking or you'd also like to own a piece of the action, you need to do it for the love and not the money.

So, what about all those people making small fortunes out of large ones? What could possibly induce people who were presumably smart enough to earn a fortune (or prudent enough to hang on to an inherited one) to blow it on a winery or a vineyard? The same thing that tempts a wine lover to pay $50, $100, $500—whatever it takes—for a bottle of wine.

We're talking intoxication here. Not from wine ethanol, but wine ethos. While too much well-aged Bordeaux can certainly render you just as inebriated as a bottle of Gallo's Thunderbird, those who get drunk on the ethos are intoxicated with the romance and lore of wine: vineyards, viticulture, enology and their people, history, culture, and landscape.

Then there are the two-hundred-plus peer-reviewed scientific papers published in the world's greatest medical journals that unanimously agree the stuff's actually good for you if you don't drink too much or too little.

It's no accident that Bacchus was a big-time Greek god, and that there is hardly a book in either the Christian or Hebrew scriptures that fails to contain at least one glowing reference to wine. Contrary to the anti-alcohol dogma of many Protestant pulpits, almost every reference to wine in the Bible is positive, with the rest being the laudable condemnation of excess.

No wonder, then, that wine has a unique ability to seduce us out of our money. But smart wine lovers can profit from the secrets of the successful and from the expensive wisdom of those who learned things the hard way. In the following pages you'll learn how to use the industry's very woes to save money buying wine to drink, and how to invest intelligently in wine and wineries, if simply drinking it doesn't satisfy your yearning to connect.

Along the way, you'll travel over vast expanses of international intrigue and back-stabbing, envy, lust, gluttony, greed, sloth, pride, wrath, blood feuds, sharp business practices, fraud, felony, deceit, high finance, low-dealing, power games, and ego trips.

That's an enormous amount of turmoil for an industry which—in its $18 billion nationwide entirety—is smaller than most individual companies in the Fortune 100.

Most people see wine as a very high-profile, glamorous product, followed by fanatical troops of jargon-spouting acolytes and debated with the same sort of contention and intensity as the latest, hottest technology product. But despite all this prominence and complexity, the wine industry is a dinky little business sector a little bit like food, a lot like entertainment, and a whole lot like agribusiness, with high costs, relatively low returns, a stagnant market, a fanatical group of neo-Prohibitionist enemies, and punitive government regulation. It experiences wild swings in prices caused by the weather, agricultural pests and diseases, foreign competition, unpredictable taxation, and fickle consumer tastes. The industry is led by a disorganized group of competing trade organizations, some headed by blood enemies—frequently resulting in fractured and ineffective leadership.

All of this enormously complicates the task of extracting a profit from wine. And even the most profitable wine businesspeople retain mere crumbs compared to the most successful in technology, food, entertainment, or agribusiness.

To put things in perspective: the entire American wine industry—all of the salaries, all of the retail wine sales, all of the commissions and distributor markups, all of the grapes, all of the sales of fertilizers and grapevines and trellis materials to the vineyards, all of the corks and bottles and labels and bottling lines and grape crushers, indeed, every cent spent or earned between the dirt and your lips—adds up to less than half the gross yearly revenues of Hewlett-Packard, *just one* successful technology company, which had gross revenues of about $43 billion in fiscal year 1997.

In contrast, the nation's largest wine trade organization, the Wine Institute of California, says that the total retail sales of all wine in the U.S., foreign and domestic, amounted to $18 billion in calendar year 1996.

You can gain another perspective by looking at the market value of publicly traded stocks. The largest wine, beer, or spirits company is Anheuser-Busch at $20.4 billion. Brown-Forman (which owns Fetzer wines but makes most of its income from bourbon and other distilled spirits) comes in second at $19.7 billion. Canandaigua Brands (once a wine company which diversified into beer and spirits) weighs in at $938 million, and the Robert Mondavi Winery at $808 million—the highest valued wine-only stock. Seagram doesn't really count because it's primarily an entertainment and spirits company which, in mid-1998, was contemplating the spinoff of its wine units into a separate company.

Compare those numbers with the most valuable companies in technology (IBM, $99.8 billion), entertainment (Disney, $57 billion), or agribusiness (Kellogg, $18.3 billion).

But even if you're the richest man in the wine business (Ernest Gallo), you're not as wealthy as those in other industries. Gallo was the only wine magnate included in *Forbes* magazine's 1997 survey of the richest four hundred people in America, and he barely made the list, tied with twenty others at number 370 and valued at $500 million. That's a far cry from Bill Gates ($40 billion), Warren Buffett ($21 billion), or any others in the top twenty, each of whom is worth $5 billion or more. What's more, it took Ernest Gallo half a century to attain this lofty position, while the founders of

Yahoo! became billionaires in less than five years.
Clearly, if making money is your goal—either as an
investor or a producer—you should not depend on
wine to do it for you.

California wines account for approximately three of
every four bottles of all wine *consumed* in the United
States. Of all the wine *produced* in the United States,
more than ninety percent comes from California, employing 112,000 people year-round and another 40,000
to 50,000 seasonal workers during harvest. Hewlett-
Packard also employs about 112,000 people (no seasonal workers), underscoring the labor-intensive nature
of wine and the resulting difficulty in getting a decent
return on investment.

Indeed, of all the public wine and wine-related
stocks, none had outperformed the Standard & Poor's
500 Index over the five years ending in mid-1998. For
the last year only, just Beringer and Canandaigua managed to beat the S&P 500.

I used Hewlett-Packard as a comparison partly because technology stock captivates people—both users
and investors—with much of the same intensity as
wine. Wine and technology are similar in many other
ways. Both kinds of companies make products that are
poorly understood by most consumers. Each has developed a fanatical cadre of geeks and jargon-meisters who
heap disdain upon the less knowledgeable (an act that
further alienates potential new customers), and both are
capital-intensive businesses centered around a technical
genius (winemaker, programmer, engineer). The wine
and technology sectors have experienced breakdowns
in the traditional three-tier sales system (manufacturer,
distributor, retailer) and have turned to direct sales as
alternatives.

But there are significant differences as well, differences that potential investors must always keep in mind.

Most significantly, nobody really *needs* wine.

You don't use it to get your work done. It won't do spreadsheets or Windows. It won't balance your checkbook (in fact, it can *un*balance it if you're not careful).

You can sell and ship a PC to anyone, anywhere in the U.S., but not a bottle of wine. Imagine where Dell Computer would be in the stock rankings if—like a winery—it could legally ship PCs only to thirteen states, and not even the ones with the most people!

Technology in the U.S. is not regulated by the government much more strictly than most other business. Wine, beer, and spirits, on the other hand, are punitively regulated according to a patchwork of irrational, antediluvian laws enforced by the federal government and fifty different states, all of which vary from one another.

Other than the Unabomber, technology has few fanatical, drooling natural enemies. But aligned against all forms of alcoholic beverages is a legion of neo-Prohibitionists: true believers composed of government bureaucrats, religious and so-called public interest groups, junk-science practitioners, and other sometimes well-meaning people who are playing with half a deck of facts and a ton of emotionally vested interests. Some of these are funded by your tax dollars, others by well-heeled foundations. But on an annual basis, they spend a sum several times larger than the annual revenues of the largest public winery, telling people not to drink any alcohol at all.

And despite a huge and conclusive body of recent

medical studies that *unanimously* agree that people who drink alcohol in moderation live longer, healthier lives than either abstainers or heavy drinkers, the neo-Prohibitionist movement carries a lot of weight in government at every level: in city councils, state legislatures, Congress, and the associated bureaucracies. Every year, the true believers in abstinence propose new taxes, restrictions on sales, and other measures designed to eliminate alcohol consumption. They do this, and are given careful consideration by government officials, despite proof that the measures they advocate do not prevent or decrease alcohol abuse, but merely serve to drive away the 92 percent of people who drink moderately, while the truly addicted continue to abuse no matter how expensive or difficult it is.

Technology and wine companies are different in one more respect. While technology firms, especially manufacturers of personal computers, have come a very long way in the past fifteen years toward making products easier to understand and use for the average consumer, wine is still dominated by geek-speaking gurus who describe wine as "round" with a smell like "old tobacco pouches left out in the Tuscan rain."

Technology companies were once very primitive when it came to marketing, but they quickly learned that just because you had a superior product didn't mean the world would beat down your doors with bales of $100 bills.

Wineries, for the most part, are still where technology companies were twenty years ago. Back in 1988, I wrote a piece for an industry newsletter, *The Wine Investor*, in which I said that to avoid becoming an endangered beverage species, wine needed to be demystified; promoted as an everyday beverage that ought to be consumed with frozen dinners, tuna casserole, and fast-food burgers.

The industry yawned then, and it still yawns as it continues to ignore the recommendations of numerous industry groups and studies that say the same thing. The Wine Market Council, formed to study and perhaps to do something about industry promotion, is ignored by most of the industry as it continually urges vintners to stop preaching to the converted and promote wine beyond the core drinker. As of mid-1998, the Wine Market Council thinks it may have received approval for a modest campaign to test some TV commercials, but even that remains doubtful. Meanwhile, the total amount of money the industry spends on advertising, adjusted for inflation, continues to drop.

The vital need for promotion brings us back to the technology comparison. Technology markets are *growing*—sometimes exponentially. Wine, on the other hand, is a stagnant market that faces a steady decline in per capita consumption. While the mid- to late 1990s saw record winery profits, those came more from increased prices than consumption. Higher prices were possible then because there were shortages of American (primarily California) wine.

But a bumper harvest in 1997 along with thousands of acres of new vineyards means that unless something is done to increase consumption, the coming five years will probably see a crash in wine prices and a resulting fall in the profit pictures of all but the most prescient wineries. The grim outlook for American wineries is aggravated by the increased market share of imported wines, especially Chilean and French, which are growing six times faster at the affordable ($5 to $10 per bottle) end of the spectrum. As domestic wineries try to

drop prices to match increased production, they are
likely to find that they cannot regain the ground they
lost when they priced themselves out of this market
segment in the mid-1990s.

In fact, when you compare the wine industry to
technology or other companies, the biggest are not as
big, the richest are not as rich, the returns not as fat,
and the opportunities not as great. But there are ways
for you to profit—for both your pocketbook and palate.
And for the end user with a wineglass, the actual operation of the product beats anything you can do with
a computer.

ONE

The Coming Shakeout in the American Wine Industry

THE CENTURY IS ABOUT TO TURN, AND AN OVERSUPPLY OF grapes and wine is causing prices and profits to plummet. Consumption is declining; depending upon which set of numbers you look at, the market is either stagnant or shrinking.

A strengthening anti-alcohol movement wants nothing less than total prohibition. Strapped for cash and spurred on by the anti-alcohol forces, Congress and other governmental bodies at every level are considering new taxes on all beverages containing alcohol.

New grapevine pests are marching through vineyards, threatening to wipe out entire vineyards, maybe an entire industry. Rising interest rates are starting to hammer wineries and vineyard owners who borrowed heavily to finance their expansion. After several years of economic good times, the wine economy seems headed for a downturn.

Welcome to the 1890s.

In the last decade of the last century, railroad baron Leland Stanford poured more than $10 million ($350 million in 1998 dollars) into the creation of the world's largest vineyard. If Viña Ranch were in operation today, at nearly 4,000 acres it would still rank as California's largest single vineyard.

Stanford, a founder of the Central Pacific Railroad (and the guy who actually hammered in the golden spike when East met West at Promontory Point, Utah, in 1869), was a giant when being part of the West meant doing things in a really big way. But even such a visionary met his downfall when he got into the wine business, and Viña Ranch was a mammoth undertaking.

The vineyards were part of a larger 59,000-acre ranch located in the hot, dusty outlands of California's Tehama County, some 130 miles north of Sacramento. At a time when westerners killed one another over water, Stanford used his immense wealth to acquire prodigious water rights for the ranch and built an elaborate system of canals and aqueducts to quench the thirst of the huge vineyard and its massive fruit orchards, cattle herds, and, of course, people.

To handle the grapes from the world's largest vineyard required the world's largest winery, which Stanford dutifully constructed, complete with newfangled incandescent electric lights and a power generation station to keep them shining. He had a railroad line built to the ranch so he could travel there in his private train car.

Money being no object, Stanford hired one of California's most respected vineyard and winery managers to handle the whole operation: Captain Hamden W. McIntyre. The former sea captain had already made his enological reputation as a key manager for Napa Valley wine pioneer Gustave Niebaum, whose Inglenook winery became one of the world's best. (Today it is regaining that reputation under the ownership of film producer Francis Ford Coppola).

Like most winery owners, then as now, Stanford held high hopes for his operation. He wanted Viña Ranch to produce table wines to rival the best of Europe, thus becoming a money machine whose sole use would be to endow the operations of Stanford University, named after his son Leland, Jr., who had died during one of the family's European vacations. But despite lavishing Viña Ranch with astounding financing and hiring the brightest and best minds of the era, Stanford was in for an education of his own.

The climate of Tehama County was too hot to grow fine wine grapes, so he took to making brandy. But a burgeoning prohibition movement and an oversupply of brandy knocked the legs out from under the selling price. An economic depression further curtailed consumption to the point that grape growers who had been selling their fruit to wineries for $14 per ton were suddenly unable to get more than $6—they were forced to sell below their cost. Despite this grim situation, Congress yielded to prohibitionist sentiments and enacted higher taxes on alcohol, making the situation even worse.

Faced with a shrinking market and plummeting prices, by 1891 the storage cellars at Viña Ranch swelled with more than 1.2 million gallons of wine and a million gallons of brandy—an inventory so large that its sheer potential for being brought to market helped depress prices further.

Stanford's company tried desperately to mitigate the disaster by exporting, and found limited success in Calcutta and Shanghai, but the amounts were too small to make a difference.

Then, as if prohibition, depression, oversupply, higher taxes, and falling prices weren't enough, a mysterious disease began to kill grapevines. Although it was never formally diagnosed, historians believe that a root louse called Phylloxera devastated the vines at Viña Ranch.

Had Leland Stanford devoted to his wine venture the same keen sense of business he had shown with the Central Pacific Railroad, he would never have pledged such enormous amounts of money to it. But the intoxication of wine's culture blinded even this rational and successful man to the reality of the world outside, a reality that consisted of:

- Decreased consumption
- Economic uncertainty
- Oversupply
- Falling prices
- Prohibitionists
- Vineyard diseases
- A lackluster export market

You might wonder why a successful industrialist such as Stanford or one of his advisers didn't see all this coming. On the other hand, with the same seven deadly afflictions coming together in the final years of this century, you could ask the same thing of today's successful vintners and growers, who seem giddy with a conviction that the good times are here to stay.

Welcome to the 1990s.

It's as if the collective consciousness of the wine industry has contracted Alzheimer's disease. There's no short-term memory of the lean times of the early 1990s, when most wineries were losing money and a record number were in bankruptcy proceedings. And there's definitely no long-term recognition of the historical disasters of the 1890s. There exists effective medicine for the current ills, just as there did a century ago. Unfortunately, the patient simply doesn't think he's sick.

Consumption is the key. Consumption is the ultimate arbiter of success or failure for any product. No matter how talented or canny management may be, there is no chance for economic success without demand. And as measured by consumption, the wine industry in the final days of the twentieth century is in sick bay.

According to statistics from the Wine Institute, wine consumption in the United States never exceeded a gallon per person until the mid-1960s. Wine was not then, nor is it today, a mainstream beverage. Until the 1950s wine in the U.S. was consumed mainly by the elite (expensive French imports), immigrant families (homemade or inexpensive domestic table wines), or skid-row alcoholics (high alcohol-fortified wines such as Gallo's Thunderbird).

The situation began to change in the 1960s when the Baby Boomer generation, then in their college years, found themselves enticed by fruity, sweet "pop" wines such as Boone's Farm, Ripple, and other beer substitutes. This generation continues to be the bulwark of today's wine consumer, a potential sales problem for wineries because younger consumers, the so-called Generation X, tend to prefer beer and spirits to wine.

Unfortunately, wine remains a marginalized beverage. Only about three-fifths of Americans drink any form of alcoholic beverage at all. Only one to two percent of the total population prefer wine to beer and spirits. In addition, a small group of core wine drinkers accounts for most of the consumption: in the U.S., only 11 percent of those preferring wine consume 88 percent of all wine.

The consumption side offers some sobering numbers. According to the Wine Institute, total U.S. wine consumption peaked in 1986. The Wine Institute statistics say Americans consumed a record 587 million gallons of wine that year, and table wines (a category that excludes sparkling and dessert wines as well as coolers and vermouth) also set a record at 487 million gallons. Not surprisingly, per capita consumption hit its all-time high of 2.43 gallons.

Consumption then went into a tailspin, dropping to 1.74 gallons per capita by 1993, when total U.S. wine consumption bottomed out at 449 million gallons, a level that resembled the late 1970s and early 1980s.

By comparison, per capita consumption exceeds 15 gallons per year in France and Luxembourg (which have the highest life expectancies in Europe), as well as Italy and Portugal.

This is the sort of pitiful market growth that would have investors in any other industry flooding their brokers with sell orders. Imagine what tech stock prices would be like if personal computer sales were the same today as they had been almost two decades ago?

The downward spiral of table wine consumption might very well have continued if not for a lucky accident. In November 1991 the CBS news magazine "60 Minutes" broadcast an episode on the so-called French Paradox. It was the first major journalistic piece exploring the reasons why the French have the longest life spans in Europe (on average four years longer than Americans) despite their less-than-healthy lifestyle, which includes smoking clouds of Gauloise cigarettes, a diet filled with paté and other fatty foods, and an allergic reaction to StairMasters and other exercise. The reason, according to the medical research, was their habit of drinking wine in moderation with meals. The CBS program revealed that research published in such journals as *The Lancet, The Journal of the American Medical Association, British Medical Journal,* and other equally respectable, peer-reviewed publications was unanimous in their conclusions that Americans and other people (not just the French) who consumed alcohol in moderation would live longer than either abstainers or heavy drinkers. The program and subsequent articles further revealed that this issue was far better documented with solid research than many other public health issues.

While this had the neo-Prohibitionists gnashing their teeth, sales of moderately priced red table wines increased as much as thirty percent in the next sixty days, causing shortages and resulting in well-known brands like Gallo's Hearty Burgundy being placed on allocation.

The resulting increase in consumer demand has helped wine consumption recover, although not to its mid-eighties peak. The Wine Institute says that per capita consumption reached 1.95 gallons in 1997, or 523 million gallons total and 462 million gallons of table wine. This is a per capita consumption approximately equal to that of 1978 and a total wine consumption comparable to 1983. It's clear that the industry will be well into the next millennium before it can match the glory days of the mid-1980s, and that consumption lag is not good news for an industry trying to outrun an impending glut.

Neither are recent supermarket wine sales data from Information Resources Inc., which show that for the 52-week period ending June 21, 1998, total table wine sales volume increased 4.2 percent, while prices rose 10.6 percent versus the previous year. In other words, prices climbed two and a half times faster than the increase in consumption.

The Robert Mondavi Winery, for example, reported that its 1997 supermarket sales grew only 2 percent by volume and 11 percent in dollars. What's more, domestic wines increased only 3 percent, while imports shot up 14.8 percent. Imports now have about 14 percent of the total market, up from 9 percent in 1995.

Despite several disorganized attempts to capitalize on the French Paradox, the U.S. wine industry has yet to stabilize itself and still looks to glory days that are more than a decade old.

The good news is that most California wineries have reported record sales and profits, in 1996 and 1997, mostly due to increases in prices that were enabled by wine shortages. The best news for the wine industry is that both total wine sales and per capita consumption are on an upward trend and perhaps, early in the next century, may equal or exceed the glory days of the mid-1980s.

Improving sales and profits, meanwhile, have distracted the wine industry from mixed signals coming from the marketplace.

The phenomenon of increasing revenues at a time

of decreasing volume for U.S. wines reflects a fundamental weakness in the market which U.S. wineries have ignored. They are blinded by higher profits resulting solely from their ability to increase prices due to a shortage of domestic wine grapes—a shortage that ended with the bumper 1997 harvest. While the effects of El Niño's rains are still uncertain in the summer of 1998, even a less-than-record harvest in California is unlikely to change the oversupply situation. This is because there are still millions of gallons of French and South African wine that can be sold into the U.S. market, along with thousands of acres of new vineyards that have begun to produce.

Wineries are ignoring the dark side of their situation, namely that their price increases have meant they have lost market share to imports. Further, the shortage that allowed them to increase prices has ended, and in the next two or three years, when they have to drop prices to compete, they will find that they have permanently lost consumers who are now loyal to imported brands.

Unless the wine industry manages to work itself out of its denial and begins to undertake substantive marketing and promotional activities, it is likely that this time period will be seen as the beginning of a serious downturn for U.S. wineries.

Industry analysts are unanimous that the 1997 bumper harvest and thousands of new acres of vineyards that are coming into production means that the next five years will see decreases in the prices for most popular priced (under $15) varietal wines—Merlot, Chardonnay, Cabernet Sauvignon—due to larger harvests, increased vineyard acreage which should start producing in commercial quantities, and the influx of high-quality imported bulk and bottled wine. While there may be some temporary shortages of grapes for expensive wines ($15 and up) it is important to recognize that this is a very small part of the market: government and private research shows that 83 percent of all wine sold in the U.S. costs less than $10 per 750ml bottle or equivalent.

This will bring good news to most consumers as prices begin to drop. More affordable prices could help increase consumption—unless the neo-Prohibitionist movement resurges to the levels of the 1980s. By summer 1998, grocery store prices in California had already begun to show dramatic competition in the less-than-$10 range with drops of two and three dollars per bottle.

On the other hand, if prices drop over the next three years at the same rate that they increased over the past three years, then it is unlikely that consumption can increase fast enough to maintain winery revenues and profits.

TWO

Why Don't People Drink More Wine?

WINE TASTES GOOD. IT ENHANCES FOOD, PROVOKES CONVERsation, and warms every gathering of family and friends where it is served. For thousands of years, the benefits of wine in moderation have been well-known by nearly every civilization. Even modern medical science has blessed its life-prolonging properties. So, given all this, why don't people drink more wine?

Mostly because the wine industry doesn't try very hard to sell it.

Each year, the wine industry spends less and less advertising its product. It fosters an image of snobbism, mystery, and formality that many consumers find offputting. The situation is further complicated by the industry's failure to capitalize upon the scientific research proving the benefits of moderate alcohol consumption.

While the National Institute on Alcohol Abuse and Alcoholism says that five to seven percent of the population cannot drink alcohol in moderation and should not drink at all, the industry has failed to make the point that moderate daily wine consumption is a good personal health decision for the remaining 93 percent.

Finally, vacillation and bitter squabbling among the major wine industry trade associations has prevented the industry from launching a generic marketing campaign such as the hugely successful ones for milk (Got Milk?), pork (the Other White Meat), beef (It's What's for Dinner), or eggs (the Incredible, Edible Egg).

Despite all evidence to the contrary, the prevailing opinion in the wine business is that if you make it, people will drink it. It's as if winemakers and sellers think they are somehow exempt from all sales and marketing factors that govern every other area of commerce. In conversations with vintner after vintner, I have come away with the impression that trying too hard to sell one's wine is somehow unseemly; one must somehow make it to the top without breaking a sweat. The ultimate success, they seem to believe, is to be found in the handful of mostly small winemakers who make a few thousand cases each year and have to beat buyers off with a grape stake, allocating a few bottles or cases of each vintage to loyal fanatics who wait patiently for years to move up the waiting list. These vintners go to extreme lengths to become unreachable, getting unlisted numbers and removing any signage from the winery property to hide from the great unwashed and unanointed.

Wine, most American winemakers think, is a privilege they bestow on civilization. The thought of having to ask someone to buy it is demeaning. This is a critical reason why wine is an increasingly marginalized beverage in America, preferred by fewer than a third of those who consume alcoholic beverages.

The industry's pitiful advertising efforts only aggravate the situation.

In 1991, all wine industry advertising in all media totaled $92 million, according to U.S. Wine Stats, an industry think tank. Adjusted for inflation, that dropped to $60 million by 1995. By comparison, Pepsico spent $1.3 billion on ads in 1995, Anheuser-Busch $577 million, and Coors $205 million. When an entire industry can't muster as much advertising as a single brand in a competing sector, you know it has a problem.

This is because wine must compete as a beverage not only with beer and spirits, but also with nonalcoholic beverages such as coffee, tea, soft drinks, and bottled water. Small wonder, then, that when most Americans think of something to drink, wine's not at the top of their list.

Of the 268 million people in the United States, there are only eleven million that the Wine Market Council defines as "core" wine drinkers, who drink wine at least two or three times per month. That's the main constituency, and things only get worse: just 9 percent of core drinkers consume wine daily; another 49 percent consume "a few times a week"; and 42 percent consume only once a week. But wine consumption is so low in the U.S. that these people account for 88 percent of all wine consumed.

Vintners talk fondly about making wine an American mealtime tradition, as it is in Europe, but the stark reality is that only about one million Americans come even close to this rosy fantasy. For the optimists, the good news is that there is ample room for improvement, if deep-seated American prejudices about wine can be overcome.

Next to the industry's lack of effort to better its market share, the greatest barrier to increased wine consumption is wine's snobby image.

Having reasoned that core wine drinkers are consuming all they're likely to, the Wine Market Council believes the greatest opportunity will be found among the twenty-one million Americans they term "marginal" wine drinkers, who drink wine once every two or three months.

Not surprisingly, the WMC's research indicates that marginal wine drinkers see wine as formal, mysterious, and intimidating. That's why they tend to save their wine consumption for restaurants, parties, and special occasions.

The formality of wine's mass appeal was firmly cemented in the seventies by the rumbling baritone of Orson Welles, who intoned in TV commercials that "We will sell no wine before its time." This slogan was intended to convey an emphasis on quality, but the impression most American consumers got instead was that wine could only be enjoyed when it "was time." While Bud and Coke are for anytime, wine has a special time—only most people don't want to be hassled with finding out when that might be.

A key reason that consumers of all sorts—even many core wine drinkers—are mystified by wine is because they are bombarded by wine writers and wineries who spend enormous amounts of time using unfathomable terminology. Consumers are told that they must learn arcane rules about which wine goes with which food and occasion, what vintages are ready to be drunk, which wines need which stemware. These writers convey the false impression that wine needs to be "understood" before it can be enjoyed.

Take the Public Broadcasting television series "Wine 101." The title of the program is intimidating by itself, implying that one needs a college course to enjoy wine. It reveals the elitist hidden within even those who profess to be egalitarian.

During a segment on appellations, Carolyn Wente of the Wente Vineyards explained that some areas with cooler climates produce wines "with a higher acid balance, but still a lot of backbone. . . ."

Acid balance? Backbone? It's meaningless nonsense for all but wine geeks. Unfortunately, this sort of jargon is easy to find. On a page of tasting notes selected at random from *Wine Spectator* magazine, I found a wine described as "young, supple, lean and trim." That could just as easily describe the latest Hollywood hardbodies. On the very same page, a Cabernet was described as "broad-shouldered, dense and tannic." The same could be said of most defensive tackles or nightclub bouncers. And what could "smooth and seductive" describe: a gigolo or politician?

How can the average wine drinker apply these terms to wine, even if so inclined? Only by learning. It's the ultimate in peer-pressure conformity: taste wine with an expert; listen to the vinobabble; the words are arcane so they must be true. Yet they offer potential wine buyers absolutely no valid information on which to base a decision.

Robert Mondavi, the father of the modern American premium wine industry, observed that when given all these rules, the American consumer says "to hell with it; give me a beer, a scotch, a cup of coffee."

There are, of course, some exceptions to the industry's inaction and promotion of mystery and formality. Fetzer's $7 million 1997 advertising campaign featured a picnic setting arranged in a pseudo-Impressionist style; Sebastiani spent $5 million in 1997 for its Na-thanson Creek brand to urge people to "plan to be spontaneous." Gallo's Ecco Domani brand told consum-ers: "Red wine is for meat. White wine is for fish. Blah! Blah! Blah! Blah! Forget the rules! Enjoy the wine." But most other Gallo advertisements promote themes counter to this, focusing instead on exotic settings (Gos-samer Bay), yuppie wine geeks (Gallo premium vari-etals), and special occasion consumption (Tott's, Balletore, Eden Roc, sparkling wines for Thanksgiving, Christmas, and New Year's).

The pioneer in promoting wine as a beverage for everyday consumption with ordinary foods is Sutter Home Winery, whose "Build a better burger" contest broke new ground in getting people to break out of the "wine as special occasion" mindset. The snobs within the wine industry, a major constituency and probably the largest single impediment to effective industry pro-motion, look down their noses upon Sutter Home and the popular, sweet-to-off-dry White Zinfandel wine cat-egory it singlehandedly invented. (Zinfandel is a red wine grape. White Zinfandel is made by removing the grape skins soon after crushing. Since the skins are the major color component in all red wines, minimizing skin contact results in a pinkish wine known elsewhere as a rosé.)

The fact that the American Dairy Farmers' "Got Milk?" campaign spent $178 million in 1996—roughly three times all wine industry advertising—points out the feeble nature of the wine industry's own individual brand advertising efforts and has helped drive industry calls for generic advertising. Unfortunately, attempts to produce some sort of "Got Wine?" campaign have faltered because of the same sort of Balkanization, backbiting, and bellyaching that has fragmented the wine industry and prevented common action in so many other areas.

At the beginning of 1999 the wine industry was as close as it has ever been to mounting a "Got Wine?" campaign. The Wine Market Council expected to launch a $1.3 million test campaign in two cities with the theme: "Wine: what are you saving it for?"

But while the industry dithers and talks urgently about the need for weaning Generation X off the milk of microbrews and flavored vodkas, time has passed it by again. Gen X is getting old. In its place is a new demographic bulge—tagged "Generation Y" or "Generation Buy" by demographers—which is nearly as large as the Boomer generation. Generation Y is defined as those people born after 1976; its leading edge attained legal drinking age in 1997. And while other savvy marketers are already aiming their sights on Gen Y and developing campaigns to attract this huge group of consumers, the wine industry is still fretting over Generation X, whose tiresome, cynical pretentiousness has gotten very old, very worn-out.

According to Cynthia Cohen, president of the Miami market research firm Marketplace 2000, Generation Y are optimistic, multicultural, and more like Boomers in their interest in quality-of-life issues such as stress and time demands. Gen Y are entrepreneurial and would rather discover new things directly with their senses than learn about them through the media. But more important to marketers of all types of goods and services, Generation Y like to buy, they don't have the practiced disdain for everything that seems to characterize Gen X. So, if you're a marketer with a finite budget, it would seem to make good business sense to concentrate on people who are receptive to your message (Generation Y) instead of those who take a perverse delight in trashing your best efforts (Gen X). The wine industry hasn't seen that the Gen Y train has already left the station while they're still waiting for Gen X to arrive.

Only time will tell if the Wine Market Council's test campaign will convince the industry to rescue itself, but its journey over the past four years has seemed much like the paradox of Zeno's turtle. In this famous Greek parable, the turtle covers half the distance to his destination each day. Even when the remaining distance can be measured in fractions of a nanometer, the sad truth is that the turtle never gets there.

But if progress is made, it must be along a path that does not promote alcohol abuse. The culture of wine can succeed where the many temperance movements of the twentieth century have failed. Prohibition clearly does not work. I believe a better model is the southern European attitude of responsibility, where children are brought up to appreciate and respect alcohol—especially wine—in a family setting.

Wine is on my family's table almost every night, so naturally it used to provoke the curiosity of my son William (as it will undoubtedly do for our new daughter). When William was about three years old, he wanted—and got—a bit of wine, a teaspoon or so, in a glass of water. He rarely took more than a sip, but it satisfied his curiosity and he soon decided that he didn't want it anymore. When he decides that he would like a sip again at the table, we'll allow that in very small amounts.

We have thought very deeply about the issue of wine and our children, and were helped by the fact that we have relatives and many close friends in Europe. It is a fact—as well as an additional paradox—that France and Italy, which have the highest per capita wine consumption in Europe, also have alcohol abuse rates that are less than one-seventh that of the U.S. or of the Scandinavian countries. Cultural differences account for this. In France and Italy, getting drunk and losing control are socially unacceptable. Youngsters are brought up with wine as just another food to be enjoyed at the family table—a far cry from alcohol as forbidden fruit, which is casually abused as an American teenage rite of passage.

THREE

Why Can't We All Just Get Along?

THE WINE INDUSTRY SUFFERS FROM EVERY POSSIBLE SCHISM, real and imagined, most of them self-inflicted. Here we see big vs. small, East vs. West, California vs. everybody else, grape growers vs. wineries, wine vs. beer and spirits, business vs. academia, domestic vs. imports, screw-tops vs. corks, distributors vs. small wineries, and on and on.

To be sure, there are some quite substantive issues that divide the wine industry, but this is a self-fragmenting organism whose divisions are maintained by massive egos, blatant hatreds, mistrust, irreconcilable personality conflicts, generational splits, disagreement over political methods, and by the congenitally cantankerous arguing for the sake of argument, thus elevating trivial differences to grander and frequently unjustified levels.

Just look at the array of groups (not counting county and local organizations) that compete for the hearts, minds, and pocketbooks of the American wine industry:

- Wine Institute of California
- American Vintners Association (AVA)
- Century Council
- Coalition for Free Trade in Licensed Beverages
- Family Winemakers of California
- Wine and Spirits Wholesalers of America
- Wine Market Council
- Women for WineSense
- AWARE (American Wine Alliance for Research and Education)

And though they have smaller wine industries, the New York State Wine and Grape Foundation, Oregon Winegrowers, and Washington Wine Institute can also have substantial impacts at the national level, especially as spoilers for the proposals of the larger organizations.

It is a rare occasion when all these groups can agree on a single issue, and even rarer when they actually cooperate. This overpopulation of wine industry organizations is not the cause of the industry's problems, but a reflection of them—and of its inability to resolve fundamental and very important differences.

The industry divisions show up as a spectacular string of economic, political, and organizational failures: the lack of a generic marketing campaign, the failure to capitalize on reams of scientific literature that agree moderate consumption is healthy, dwindling federal export support to counter foreign subsidies, a lack of political clout, failure to present a unified effort on direct shipping, and more.

As with most aspects of the American wine industry, E. & J. Gallo, the country's largest winery, is the defining presence. Gallo is often an active contributor to the turmoil, but more often it lets the internecine wars rage unabated, reasoning that the troubles of others can only help preserve its market dominance.

While the Wine Institute disingenuously tries to deny its overwhelming influence, Gallo—as the Institute's largest single contributor—clearly controls the nation's largest wine trade organization. Indeed, most industry splinter groups were formed as a reaction against Gallo's hegemony over the Wine Institute and the institute's domination of the industry's voice.

In the technology sector, successful companies have exercised leadership to develop the market, incubate fledgling firms, and provide opportunities for them. While some of these companies have grown to near-monopolies in the process, they realize that a growing market provides profits for a lot more people.

Instead, Gallo has maintained a Cold War mentality, not exercising leadership, not helping to grow the customer base. Instead, it has concentrated on maintaining its position in a shrinking market by trying to stifle competition. This counterproductive attitude has left a leadership vacuum in the wine industry, and that alone is responsible for much of the chaos. In addition, Gallo's brass-knuckle tactics and its propensity for making high-alcohol misery wines aggressively marketed to skid-row alcoholics has fostered an atmosphere of distrust by the rest of the wine industry that borders on paranoia.

The disruptive effects appear most vividly in the

case of the aforementioned Wine Institute of California, the pre-eminent U.S. wine trade organization. Founded in 1934, it represents a little more than 400 of California's 750 wineries (figures are hard to come by because the institute will not release precise numbers). But among those 400 wineries are the ones that count: Gallo, United Distillers and Vintners (the former Heublein), Beringer, and other industry heavyweights. Gallo alone pays close to $2 million of the institute's $5 million annual budget. But the institute's domination by Gallo and other very large wineries means that their interests come first, whether or not it is to the detriment of the smaller winery members.

The most cataclysmic event in the Wine Institute's recent history began in April 1990 with a rebellion by a number of members, including Robert Mondavi, over the California Wine Commission, established by the state legislature in 1985 as a self-taxing marketing order dedicated to promoting wine consumption. Because Gallo and other large California wineries dominate the political scene with hefty campaign contributions and lobbying muscle, the CWC favored Gallo, to the disadvantage of smaller wineries, and funded an ill-conceived concept that only helped marginalize wine instead of broadening the market.

CWC dues were based on the prices of grapes—meaning that smaller, premium wineries which used finer grapes paid much more in proportion to their size than did the large wineries. Premium wineries like Robert Mondavi and the rebellion's ringleaders, Bill MacIver (Matanzas Creek) and Brice Jones (Sonoma-Cutrer), were paying $1,500 per ton and higher for expensive Napa, Sonoma, and other North Coast grapes, while

Gallo was buying lower quality Central Valley grapes for $250 to $400 per ton.

However, because the legislature designated the Wine Institute as administrator of the CWC's funds, MacIver and his supporters charged that Gallo's interests came first. The dissidents then forced a new election on the marketing order in 1990 and abolished the commission. "The CWC election was a referendum on the Wine Institute," said MacIver, who, along with Brice Jones and others, soon afterward formed an alternative organization for California vintners, the Family Winemakers of California.

For years after the commission's demise, the Wine Institute's long-time executive director, John DeLuca, complained to anyone who would listen that the vote was unjust because even though a clear majority of all the wineries in California voted to abolish the CWC, 89 percent of the industry *by volume* had voted to continue the marketing order. MacIver would respond that this was just the point. Over the next year, the Wine Institute's membership would drop by almost thirty percent. The Wine Institute has never recovered from the defections of 1990-91, a key fact that led to layoffs of almost one-fourth of its staff in 1994.

The vote on the CWC might have come to a different conclusion if the promotional campaigns it funded had been well-conceived and well-executed. But instead of creating a campaign that would expand the market for wine, the CWC's major thrust was to train wine service personnel in restaurants. What better way to convince people that wine is a special occasion beverage that should not be consumed at home? Instead of making a larger tent to hold more people, the CWC concentrated on gilding the tent poles.

Critics of the CWC say that the focus on restaurants came because Gallo, which had terrific presence on store shelves, had little space on restaurant wine lists. Gallo feared that an industry marketing campaign encouraging everyone to drink wine in general would result in greater retail sales of other wineries' products and a loss of market share for the Modesto mammoth. This concern was no doubt an important factor in 1993, when Bob Gallo (Julio's son) refused to meet with the Family Winemakers of California, representatives of the Enology Department at UC Davis, and others to discuss the creation of a new commission to fund research.

The Wine Institute's positions on many other key industry issues and programs shows that it takes care of Gallo and its other large winery members first. For example, the Wine Institute administers the California portion of wine export subsidies appropriated by the Department of Agriculture's Market Promotion Program (MPP). This program is designed to counter the subsidies that most other countries provide to their farmers, thus providing a level export playing field for American agricultural producers. At its height from 1986–1991, the Wine Institute allocated about $67 million in MMP funds to California wineries, with the majority going to E. &. J. Gallo. In 1991 alone, the Wine Institute gave Gallo a little more than $5.1 million out of the $10.1 million allotted for all California wineries. While it is true that Gallo produces about one-third of California wine, getting one-half of the funds is disproportionately high—especially when no one will release data on what proportion of exports Gallo accounts for.

Critics both inside and outside of the wine industry called this "welfare for the rich," a factor which, combined with the Wine Institute's dwindling political influence in Washington, has resulted in dramatic cuts to the wine segment of the MPP. In 1997 total wine industry MPP funds dropped to $1.89 million, with Gallo receiving just $530,000 of that.

The long-term, multi-million-dollar MPP subsidy to Gallo over the years has probably done more to hurt exports of American wines and their international image than it has done to help. This is because the products that Gallo has used these funds to export and promote have tended to be cheap, second-rate, jug-style wines, rather than the premium wines that represent the best the U.S. has to offer. But because of the money subsidizing Gallo's efforts, most—if not all—of the American wines found in many foreign outlets are Gallo brands.

In 1990, the California legislature's Senate Committee on Taxation and Revenue considered a bill to levy an additional tax on misery wines (those artificially boosted with pure alcohol so the buyer can get drunk faster) and to differentiate them from expensive ports and dessert wines (which are rarely abused). Thanks to heavy lobbying, the bill quietly died in committee. While Gallo and Canandaigua profit from wines made for the express purpose of getting people intoxicated, the vast majority of vintners support higher taxes and greater controls on these wines because they don't want their premium products tainted by association with the likes of Thunderbird and Richard's Wild Irish Rose.

Most premium wineries were livid when they found out that the primary opponent of the bill to tax skid-row wines in California was—the Wine Institute. It was even a surprise to some small winery members on the institute's own executive committee, who had never been told of the organization's position on the bill. It was lost on no one that Gallo was the *only* California winery at the time to benefit.

To be sure, there is a new generation of Gallos (Matt and Gina) who are making fine wine from their vast holdings in Sonoma County and deserve the respect of both winemakers and wine drinkers. But despite their ubiquity in Gallo's advertising, they have little power in the wine empire, which is controlled with an iron fist from Modesto by Ernest and his son Joe.

For example, the decision to radically recontour (some say "strip mine") some of the beautiful hills in Sonoma County's Dry Creek Valley in order to make it easier to plant vineyards, came from Modesto. Biologists say the increased soil runoff will ruin prime salmon and steelhead spawning streams and possibly increase flooding along the Russian River, which has already experienced two devastating floods in the past five years. As of early 1998, the resulting public outcry delayed the intended actions and prompted the County Board of Supervisors to consider new laws that would prevent similar actions.

Certainly Gallo is shrewd enough to recognize the value of good PR and relations with its poorer cousins when it comes to minor issues. When it doesn't really matter, Gallo will yield to the institute's smaller members. But the Wine Institute simply cannot take action on any major issue that runs counter to Gallo's interests—even if it is in the long-term worst interest of the institute or the industry.

The Wine Institute's president, John DeLuca, succeeded for a long time in creating more influence for the wine industry than its relatively small market share would merit. A product of the old school of LBJ Democratic politics, in which the art of the possible was preferred to the dream of the ideal, DeLuca has probably done a better job than any other person could of reconciling the interests of small wineries in the institute with the Gallo presence. But as the schism of the early 1990s has shown, the industry divisions are so great and the influence of the Gallos so overpowering that even DeLuca has had an increasingly difficult time bridging the chasms. The Market Promotion Program, for example, has been nearly destroyed because Gallo hogged most of the funds and made such a large and easy target for critics. This is why there are so many other wine industry organizations that will continue to exist so long as the industry's goliath, Gallo, remains arrogantly at odds with the vast majority of America's vintners.

Nothing better illustrates the Laurel and Hardy nature of the wine industry's trade organizations than the short-lived National Wine Appreciation Week. Introduced with the fervor of a Chautauqua revival in 1993, this event was touted by every trade group from the Wine Institute to the American Vintner's Association as the beginning of a new day of united action, peace, and love—an annual event that would help focus public attention on the positive aspects of wine and help the industry fight its public policy battles.

Wine Appreciation Week was such an important event that everybody involved jockeyed to take as much credit for it as possible. Institute president DeLuca, for example, said that a meeting with President Clinton during Wine Appreciation Week was responsible for the President's spring 1993 statement on MTV that "there's some evidence that wine, for example, is good for your heart. . . ." DeLuca and others claimed that the industry's united action also helped derail new taxes on wine.

Very important. Much accomplished. Highly valuable.

So how come, a year later, Wine Appreciation Week 1994 was the week that wasn't? It turns out that this new United Nations of Wine was more like the League of Nations. In 1994, Americans could celebrate National Scleroderma Week, National Good Teen Day, National Commodore John Barry Day, National Geography Awareness Week, and a host of other special, congressionally sanctioned commemorations.

But not Wine Appreciation Week. Not again. Not since.

This valuable, terribly important event, the shining beacon of industry unity, harbinger of the new era of wine industry cooperation, slipped away like a forgotten New Year's resolution.

The old schisms divided the industry; each organization was so certain that it and it alone was responsible for the event's initial success that they saw no need to cooperate further. The only thing the various trade organizations could agree upon concerning the failure to promote a 1994 Wine Appreciation Week was that they all had more important things to do.

It is clear from looking at the articles in the general media and from reactions from public policy makers that the 1993 Wine Appreciation Week made a significant impact on both the public and those who conduct the public's business. This week was a very good example of what the industry can do if they all decide to read from the same page. But, sadly, the egos involved are too big and the willingness to compromise and cooperate is too small to sustain any sort of unified action and the organizational fault lines continue to widen.

The great divide in California—Wine Institute vs. the Family Winemakers of California—mirrors the Gallo versus the world reality. A similar chasm exists at the national level with Gallo and its proxy, the Wine Institute, squaring off against the American Vintners Association (AVA).

Located in Washington, D.C., the AVA represents more wineries than any other organization, approximately 530 in forty-one states. But while the AVA counts a handful of large wineries among its members—Canandaigua, Sebastiani, Mondavi, Wente, Wine Alliance—the vast majority of AVA members are mostly non-California wineries with smaller sales and market share. As a result, the AVA struggles to maintain a national presence and retain its members on a budget of about $500,000 and a staff of four people. While there are more than 1,600 wineries in forty-seven U.S. states (about 750 in California), less than a third are members of the AVA.

The AVA grew quickly in the early 1990s, in large part as a reaction against national political efforts by the Wine Institute to advance the agendas of large corporate wineries such as Gallo, Beringer, United Distillers & Vintners, which were contrary to the interests of small, mostly family-owned wineries. In general, these small wineries supported (and the Wine Institute either opposed or failed to support):

1. An aggressive campaign to promote the health effects of moderate wine consumption
2. Small-winery tax exemptions
3. Direct shipping of wine from wineries to consumers in other states
4. Aggressive industry marketing promotions

While the AVA has had some small victories, most notably the launch of the Wine Market Council, the lack of support from larger wineries has kept its budget low and its overall impact small. In addition, the AVA's Cellarmaster shipping system ranks as the organization's biggest failure and is probably responsible for most of AVA membership losses in 1997.

Cellarmaster was intended to be a way for AVA members to ship their wines legally to consumers in all fifty states. While one group of members decided to fight the legality of direct shipping regulations, Cellarmaster was designed to fit into the laws and regulations that support the old, decaying three-tier system: producer to wholesaler to retailer. The result was an expensive, confusing system that, as of January 1998, was shipping wines from exactly *two* American wineries into less than a dozen states.

In addition, the very philosophy of Cellarmasters— to support and work within the three-tier system—was anticonsumer because of its high prices and lack of choice, and ran counter to some of the AVA's strongest patrons, who support legal challenges to restrictions on direct shipping rather than trying to work within an antiquated system whose time, they say, has long passed.

Some of the more vocal challengers of the three-tier sales and distribution system are the same ones who overthrew the California Wine Commission and later formed the Family Winemakers of California. Bill MacIver, for one, co-owner of Sonoma's Matanzas Creek Winery, was a founding father of both the FWC and the cutting edge of an organization called the Coalition for Free Trade, which has successfully challenged prohibitions on direct shipping into a number of key states.

A candid, passionate, quick-witted, and sharp-tongued advocate of his causes, MacIver believes that the AVA inflicted serious damage on itself by making Cellarmasters such an expensive and unwieldy abomination, and by spending too little time addressing its members' needs and too much time trying to appease the interests of the Wine and Spirits Wholesalers Association. As its name indicates, this group represents the middle segment of the three-tier system that direct shipping is designed to circumvent. This new feud, which threatens to unravel many of the AVA's gains (and is causing members to flee), is an example of how inside-the-beltway thinking can sabotage the best of intentions.

If the Wine Institute and the AVA and CFT and the FWC were the only organizations at each other's throats, the task of reconciliation and unity might be possible. But there are more, a lot more, each with its own dogmatic reasons not to cooperate with the others.

An arm of the distilled spirits industry, the Century Council, probably holds the record for wasting more money than any other alcoholic beverage trade group in history. It began in 1991 with a $40 million war chest to support community drunk driving campaigns and fight underage drinking. From the beginning, it got no support from large beer companies such as Anheuser-Busch and Miller, and almost none from the wine industry. Mondavi was the only American winery among the founders that was not owned by a distilled spirits organization.

Most American wineries have a dislike of spirits companies that frequently slips into loathing. The lightning rod for that loathing is usually DISCUS (Distilled Spirits Council of the U.S., Inc.), representing U.S. producers and marketers of distilled spirits. Vintners frequently disparage spirits as "booze," and tend to go thermonuclear over the successful campaign by DISCUS and its most prominent member, Seagram, over "equivalency," or the concept that a drink of wine, beer, and spirits are the same because they contain the same amount of alcohol.

While technically accurate, this oversimplification ignores the documented differences in drinking patterns associated with each type of beverage. If you factor out misery wines such as Gallo's Thunderbird, ample evidence shows that wine is overwhelmingly a beverage of moderation, most often consumed with food and in smaller quantities. Scores of research studies indicate that wine drinkers have an edge for health and longevity over beer and spirits drinkers. Since these studies show that alcohol is the primary ingredient responsible for this beneficial health effect, researchers agree that wine, beer, and spirits are all about the same as inherently healthy beverages. Wine simply tends to be consumed in a more moderate fashion. For example, in 1988 the U.S. Justice Department found table wine implicated in just over one percent of drunk driving accidents.

With this history of animosity between wine and distilled spirits producers, it's no wonder that the wine industry looked askance at the spirits-funded Century Council. The council, in turn, tried to buy respectability and cloak itself in the warm fuzzies of wine's image by hiring away Patricia Schneider, founding executive director of the American Wine Alliance for Research and Education (AWARE), yet another industry group, this one overseen by doctors and other medical professionals in 1989 who wanted to inform people and the health industry about the proliferation of research pertaining to the French Paradox. Schneider had resigned as head of the Wine Institute's Research and Education Department because she and the founders, including attorney John Hinman, vintner MacIver, and retailer Jerome Draper, believed that the institute was not devoting adequate resources to the health issue.

AWARE never really got off the ground because it only received lukewarm support from the wine industry. Of the 1,600 wineries in America, only about a hundred joined AWARE. This lack of widespread industry enthusiasm was a major factor in Schneider's resignation from AWARE in 1993. By 1995, with physicians still mostly as clueless about the French Paradox as they were six years earlier, AWARE vanished in all but name, into the American Vintners Association, which has done nothing with it since.

Another group, Women for WineSense, was formed in 1992 by Julie Williams (Frog's Leap) and Michaela Rodeno (St. Supéry), women working in the wine industry. It was founded primarily to help counter the false and misleading, tax-supported propaganda in schools that equated Chardonnay with cocaine and winemakers with Colombian drug lords. Overall, WWS probably has all its prospective heads screwed on tighter than any other wine industry organization. Unlike most other groups, they have shown a willingness to compromise and to desire progress over short-term or ideological goals. If there was any glue at all in the first and only Wine Appreciation Week, it was Women for Winesense, who seem able to look beyond schoolboy fisticuffs and recognize that there are more important battles to be won. It's unfortunate that there are not more women in the wine industry, and even sadder that there are so terribly few women in positions of real power at E. & J. Gallo, Beringer, Mondavi, Canandaigua, Diageo (the former Heublein), Sebastiani, Kendall-Jackson, Franzia, and other large wineries.

These few selected examples of the wine industry's continuing flood of self-defeating behavior shows that without leadership from market leader Gallo and its proxy, the Wine Institute, the various fragments of the American wine industry will continue to follow a dozen prophets in different directions, most of which will not lead to the promised land of a bottle of wine on every American table every night. But vintners are nothing if not an existential bunch of people, and they find meaning in doing, even if the doing seems like a hopeless cause.

If you're looking at the wine industry as an investment, knowing it's Balkanized nature will help you assess events. Since the industry cannot mount a concerted effort for almost anything, it will be helpless at creating a promotional campaign to help increase consumption and prevent grape-glut-driven price drops—good for buying wine, bad for buying wine stocks. The same holds true for the gathering onslaught of neo-Prohibitionist attacks on alcohol in general, which are likely to stifle or moderate consumption increases.

FOUR

The $4 Billion Disaster that Didn't Have to Happen

ALL OVER CALIFORNIA WINE COUNTRY, HULKING, GNARLED mounds of grapevines are being bulldozed into funeral pyres as big as two-story houses; they stand in the middle of bare-dirt fields, smoldering the ashes of lost dreams into the sky.

Reverdy Johnson saw his wine country dream go up in smoke simply because he trusted viticultural experts at the University of California at Davis. Johnson, a former president of the Napa Valley Vintners Association and a successful San Francisco attorney, started a winery in 1977 with an equally influential architect and friend, William Turnbull, Jr. They planted the highly recommended grapevines that the UC Davis experts recommended. Fifteen years later they had to sell their winery, its finances crippled by grapevines having fallen victim to a vineyard pest that the experts said had been tamed.

Like Johnson, other owners of California wine-grape vineyards are, even today, needlessly borrowing a sum that could easily exceed $4 billion because ignorant university researchers and clueless bankers forced California grape growers to plant their vineyards with the wrong type of grapevine. The researchers and bankers did this despite repeated warnings from internationally recognized French and American researchers that the grapevine—called AxR1—could not resist attacks from Phylloxera, a tiny louse that feeds on the roots of wine grapevines and gradually kills them.

Since the early 1990s, the wine press and the general media have lamented the disastrous spread of the tiny vine insect that devastated the world of wine almost exactly a century before and began again in earnest in California in about 1980.

When Phylloxera attacks a vine, the quality of the juice from the grapes is not affected for the first couple of years; but year after year the vines produce less and less fruit, until the grapes fail to ripen properly and can't be used for premium wine; eventually they die. There is no effective treatment and no known cure except to rip out the vine and replace it with a new one, which hopefully can resist the bug.

Replacing an acre of wine grapes costs about $25,000. A new vineyard will have at least three nonproductive years until it finally bears a commercial-level crop. If an average acre produces 4.5 tons of grapes and those grapes can be sold for $1,200 per ton, that means a loss to the vineyard owner of $5,400 per year, or about $16,200 over the three nonproductive years. Figure in the replanting costs, and pulling out and replanting a Phylloxera-infested vineyard can easily cost a farmer more than $40,000 per acre.

In California there are 85,000 acres of wine grapes susceptible to Phylloxera, and most of them will eventually have to be replaced. The costs of cultivating and maintaining the new vineyards each nonproductive year plus the interest expense on the borrowed funds to replant, easily push the total cost over the $4 billion mark. Some premium growers, like Agustin Huneeus, owner of Franciscan Vineyards, assert that the true cost is closer to $70,000 per acre, which would make this a $6 billion disaster.

The outlook is just as grim when a Phylloxera-hammered grower gives up and tries to sell. The 1996 Napa Valley Economics Survey found that buyers were willing to pay about $40,000 per acre of vineyard planted on Phylloxera-resistant rootstock, but less than half that for vineyards planted with AxR1.

None of this had to happen. The information on AxR1's vulnerability to Phylloxera was well-documented and has been known to the French for almost a century. But as the saying goes, "There are none so blind as those who will not see."

The roots of this situation date to the 1860s, when an unknown malady began to kill the vineyards of France. By the time scientists puzzled through the situation and discovered Phylloxera was the cause, six million acres—almost half of all French vineyards—had been destroyed.

The solution—grafting the tops (called scions) of French vines (Vitis vinifera) onto American rootstock—was, and still seems to be, ironically galling for the French. Native North American grapes don't make terribly good wine, but their roots resist attacks from the sap-sucking Phylloxera bugs. The grafted result is a relatively good coat-hanger-and-duct-tape solution that has lasted for more than a century.

Today, French vinifera scions grafted to American rootstock are the world standard. Chile and large parts of Australia are the only major wine growing regions that have not yet suffered an invasion of Phylloxera; experts say their turn is inevitable.

All of this would be no further problem except for efforts to increase grape production and resistance to other pests and diseases. The vines that produce wine grapes are subject to a plethora of insects, viruses, fungi, nematodes (tiny soil worms), and other enemies so numerous it's a wonder they can survive at all.

So, in a quest to produce a vine that resists the maximum number of pests and also produces the maximum quantity of good wine, scientists began crossbreeding various rootstocks and testing them in the vineyard. They came up with a dizzying array of rootstocks with names like St. George, Freedom, Harmony, but more often a more prosaic babble of alphanumeric soup such as SO4, 140Ru—and AxR1.

Despite the availability of genetic engineering techniques in other areas of agriculture, the lack of adequate wine research means that rootstock manipulation today is, for the most part, more like canine pedigree breeding, stuck back in the Luther Burbank/Mendelian days. Thanks to the tiny size of the wine industry and an even smaller enology and viticulture research establishment, it is a trial-and-error process, with the emphasis on error.

One of the biggest errors began, unnoticed, in the 1950s and 1960s, when researchers at UC Davis concluded that the AxR1 rootstock was ideal for California.

It seemed to fit the state's hot, dry climate, gave grape yields that were sometimes twice that of other rootstocks, and had a broad resistance to pests, especially Phylloxera—or so they thought.

UC Davis promoted AxR1 heavily by recommending its planting through farm agents. Banks that loaned to the wine industry began to require AxR1 rootstock as a precondition for obtaining loans. By 1980, AxR1 had become the most popular rootstock in California, with a sixty-plus percent share of the market in the ultrapremium Napa and Sonoma regions.

Unknown to the banks, vineyard owners, and farm advisers who blindly relied upon the UC Davis recommendations, French researchers had known since 1897 that AxR1 contained some genes from the original vinifera vines that were devastated by Phylloxera. Starting in about 1908, Phylloxera ate AxR1's lunch in France, South Africa, Algeria, and Sicily. Before 1920 rolled around, French, Italian, and other viticultural experts knew conclusively that AxR1 was definitely *not* Phylloxera resistant.

It's hard to determine whether the UC Davis researchers were simply unaware of the French research, negligent, or incompetent in refusing to pay attention to these very clear results. Some observers believe there was a California arrogance at work, that somehow it was felt that what had failed all over the world would work here. "I think it's an American phenomenon that despite the evidence, we still think we're different," Napa Valley vineyard consultant Rich Nagaoka told *Wine Spectator* magazine.

Throughout this period, French researchers and Americans who studied the French (and Italian and South African) experience with AxR1 continually cautioned UC Davis on AxR1, to no avail. In 1979, Lucie Morton, a consulting viticulturalist who studied at France's National Agricultural University in Montpellier, wrote an article in the trade journal *Wines & Vines* warning that AxR1 was not Phylloxera resistant. Then as today, she was dismissed as alarmist or, worse, a Francophile, because she studied in France under one of the world's greatest viticultural authors and professors, Dr. Pierre Galet. No one paid attention six years later when *Wines & Vines* reprinted the article at Morton's urging—despite the fact that Phylloxera had actually appeared on AxR1 vines in 1980 in a vineyard in Napa Valley's Rutherford area. Unable to admit that they had committed a grave mistake by recommending AxR1 so heavily, UC Davis researchers went into denial/stonewalling mode, insisting that the problem vines weren't AxR1 at all.

For five years UC Davis researchers and their allies continued to cover up the growing problem and their own culpability in promoting it. In an August 6, 1985, memo, a "Phylloxera Task Force" composed of UC Davis experts and county agricultural agents in Napa, Sonoma, and Lake counties continued to recommend AxR1 as "a highly productive and Phylloxera resistant rootstock."

But by 1991 towering funeral pyres of Phylloxera-afflicted vines ripped from afflicted fields and set ablaze to clear way for replanting began appearing all across Napa and Sonoma wine country. These bonfires burned up more than the ravaged vines—they consumed the hopes of growers, charred the implicit trust that the industry had once placed in UC Davis, and destroyed the last chance that UC Davis had to sweep the problem under the rug. But the academics had been shoving

AxR1 into the pipeline so aggressively that it was hard to shut off the faucet. Grapevine nurseries, which invested millions in selling AxR1 to growers, were continuing to promote AxR1 to avoid the financial losses entailed by scrapping their inventories. So they unloaded their damaged goods and passed the losses on to growers.

The situation became so bad that in May 1991 a stern memo went out to all California grapevine nurseries from Jim Wolpert, Cooperative Extension viticulturalist at UC Davis and chair of the Phylloxera Task Force (new to the group since its 1985 endorsement of AxR1): "It has come to our attention that some grapevine nurseries are continuing to promote the use of AXR#1 rootstock . . . AXR#1 is NO LONGER [his capitalization] a viable rootstock . . . My concern here is . . . with the ACTIVE PROMOTION of AXR#1 by anyone within the nursery industry. It is bad viticulture; and in my opinion it is ultimately bad business. Any nursery continuing to promote AXR#1 rootstock as 'resistant' to Phylloxera risks its good reputation."

The issue blew up into full public controversy in 1992 when I translated an article from the *La Revue d'Enologie* by Dr. Galet, then-vice-chairman of the Viticulture Department at Montpellier, in an issue of my publication, *Wine Business Insider*. The use of AxR1, Galet said, has been abandoned in France "a long time ago because of its poor performance [Phylloxera resistance], already known in 1902 by [Louis] Ravez in his book on American vines."

Certainly, competent researchers should have been aware of the work by Galet, Ravez, and others, just as they should have been aware of AxR1's spectacular failures wherever it had been used in the world. Knowing these basic and prominent facts would have been a prudent act of due diligence that could have avoided the $4 billion mistake. But even if they had been unaware of the research, UC Davis and other researchers had the issue presented to them bluntly by Galet in a way that any prudent person could not ignore.

"During my first trip to California [1980]," Galet's article read, "I tried very assertively to bring the dangers of [AxR1] to the attention of Napa Valley viticulturists and UC Davis professors, but without success. Their new vineyards continue to be planted on [AxR1] because UC Davis are proprietors of fields of mother vines." This last was a reference to the university's Federal Plant Materials Service (FPMS), which is supposed to be a source of high quality, disease-free rootstock which is sold to commercial vine nurseries.

Conflict of interest charges have hovered over UC Davis for two decades now. Perhaps the conflict of interest is emotional rather than economic. Most people running grapevine nurseries studied under the same UC Davis professors who originally made the $4 billion fumble. Some at UC Davis had family members who owned rootstock nurseries.

In addition, UC Davis invested tremendous resources in AxR1 for FPMS in the 1970s and 1980s, a powerful bureaucratic incentive to ignore seventy-five years of French research in general and the opinionated Dr. Galet in particular. This "Not Invented Here" syndrome would cost California grape growers dearly, especially with the massive boom in new vineyard plantings—almost all on AxR1—that took place in the 1980s.

Galet's 1991 article pointed out that "in 1990 I returned to California to tour the sick vineyards, and dur-

ing a four-hour seminar before 300 owners, growers
and winery managers . . . made an urgent appeal for
good rootstock, but the American technicians at UC
Davis . . . opposed the introduction of plants coming
from France. They even resorted to the old—and false—
theory of the German Borner (1910) that two types of
Phylloxera existed, one of which was more aggressive
than the other. It is my opinion that they have adopted
this in order to cover up their incompetence. . . ."

Galet's reference here was to UC Davis assertions
that Phylloxera had unexpectedly mutated into a more
virulent form called Biotype B. The development of a
more powerful mutant strain of Phylloxera would, of
course, be the perfect way to excuse the UC Davis failure to note earlier French research and of Galet's recent warnings.

While a number of other universities and research
establishments—including Galet's—agree that there are
different biotypes of Phylloxera, the scientific consensus
that developed over the next five years concluded that
there wasn't enough difference among the biotypes to
account for the spectacular failure of AxR1, a failure
that all now agree was due to vinifera genes.

Today, even UC Davis researchers admit that AxR1
failed to resist Phylloxera because it contains vinifera
genes. "Biotypes are irrelevant to the collapse of AxR1,"
UC Davis researcher Andy Walker told the *New York
Times* in 1993.

But in early 1992 anyone who dared challenge UC
Davis found themselves in for a heap of abuse. Few of
the few people responding to Galet's comments actually
addressed the issue at hand. Instead, the typical response was that of Justin Meyer, owner of Silver Oak
Cellars and then-president of the American Vineyard

Foundation, who said that Galet's charges "ring of French arrogance and fear of the quality and success of California wines, which are much due to UC Davis." Meyer added that perhaps the emergence of Biotype B was aided by the drought that affected California in the late 1980s and early 1990s, something that "could not be foreseen by scientific research."

Funding for enology and viticulture research lags because the University of California system will not underwrite it and the industry won't open its own checkbook. The American Vineyard Foundation—a private group set up to beg for research funds—relies upon voluntary contributions, and in most years can't manage to scrape together a million dollars. This anorexic budget means that, while staffing levels vary, UC Davis rarely has more than four or five full-time researchers in enology and viticulture. Galet's research institute, by contrast, has seventy-five full-time scientists at Montpellier alone. In addition, there are several times that many scattered among other French universities. Even the fledgling Australian wine industry, less than one-third the size of America's, spends more than $7 million per year on research.

Looked at another way, if the industry had managed to pony up just one percent of the eventual $4 billion tab for the Phylloxera disaster, it would have provided $40 million in research. That amount could easily have paid for higher quality researchers who would probably have spotted AxR1's vinifera genes before they became a viticultural pipe bomb.

Voluntary contributions aren't sufficient, and even attempts to fund research through assessments on the sale of vines have met with opposition and court challenges. A proposal by the California legislature to create

the California Grape and Wine Research Commission
in the early 1990s was beaten back by the same coalition
of wineries that successfully fought for the dismantling
of the California Wine Commission. This group contended that the proposal unfairly taxed them without
giving them a sufficient voice in the group's operation.

Today, only about one in seven of the 4,000 California vineyards and 750 wineries contributes to the AVF.
The rest are getting a free ride. They don't recognize
that the bus may let them off in the same place it did
with AxR1.

A small effort began in 1993 when grapevine nurseries decided to tax themselves for rootstock research
and successfully created the California Grape Rootstock
Improvement Commission, which levies a small tax on
the forty or so companies that grow and sell vines. That
tax raised about $250,000 in 1996 and is being chal-
lenged by the Duarte Nursery in Hughson, California,
which contends the assessment is a violation of its constitutional rights. The Duarte case suffered a setback in
1997 when the U.S. Supreme Court ruled that such industry self-taxation schemes are constitutional. The
nursery said it will continue the litigation.

The best spin on the $4 billion Phylloxera debacle
is that, well, vineyards have to be replanted eventually
anyway, and just look at how much more productive
the vineyards will be when redone with new trellises,
vine spacing, and other modern techniques. Andy Beck-
stoffer, one of California's largest vineyard owners and
operators, has this perspective: "If you replant 18,000
acres between 1990 and 2000, that's business as usual.
If it's done in three years, that's a serious problem."
Others have compared it to the difference between

making monthly mortgage payments and facing a balloon payment for the entire balance, without warning.

If Phylloxera were the only problem that vineyard owners faced, life would be good. But there are more pests lined up to devastate a vineyard than the grower has arrows in his quiver. While it's hard to pick the most dangerous ones out of a lineup, "Black Goo" and Pierce's Disease seem to have elbowed their way to the front of the line.

Black Goo is a new and mysterious killer stalking California vineyards and the rest of the world. Its victims? Mere toddlers, two or three, sometimes even seven years old. Ironically, these are mostly the same vines that were recently planted to replace those choked off by Phylloxera.

Vines affected with Black Goo show stunted growth, leaf yellowing and curling—symptoms that mimic aspects of other vine problems—Pierce's Disease, viral infections, even poor vineyard practices. But when the vine is cut transversely below the grafting union, a dark goo oozes from the small vessels that carry water and nourishment from the roots to the stems, leaves, and grapes. In France, Italy, New Zealand, and South Africa the mystery disease most often manifests itself as a slow decline that gradually makes the vineyards unprofitable. In the very hot climates of California and Australia, its effects can come much quicker: one day the vine looks fine, the next it's dead. Viticulturists began seeing the disease in quantity about 1993, working much like atherosclerosis in humans, killing slowly or suddenly, depending upon stress.

Very little else is known, not even whether Black Goo is a relatively minor, self-limiting disease that stages Ebola-like raids from the ecological fringes, or the first signs of a geometrically spreading epidemic that could rival or surpass the multi-billion-dollar worldwide devastation caused by Phylloxera.

The stakes are very high: Phylloxera-affected grape growers who have gone deeply in debt to replant their vineyards say that a new disease affecting their replanted vines could mean bankruptcy.

Lucie Morton, the original AxR1 whistleblower and now a Virginia-based vineyard consultant and ampelographer (expert in identifying grapevine varieties), first brought the disease to the attention of the American wine industry. She said she spotted the black goo with increasing frequency as she visited her consulting clients to advise them on which rootstocks to plant in vineyards wiped out by Phylloxera.

In 1993, when Morton made the rounds of wine industry trade shows with samples of the disease, she was again branded an alarmist and her findings were dismissed because she is a hands-on vineyard consultant rather than a laboratory scientist. Companies providing rootstock for vineyards, a number of local agricultural authorities, and researchers at UC Davis contended that what Morton was showing around was neither a threat nor a new disease, but some form of known problem such as Esea or the results of poor grafting, vineyard practices or some latent virus, all of which, they said, could cause forms of dark streaking in grapevine tissues.

Each of the thirteen vineyard managers interviewed for this chapter said they had seen the disease in new vines in their own or someone else's vineyard, and every one of them indicated that they thought the problem was increasing. "Nobody wants to admit they have it," said one large vineyard owner. "After the Phyllox-era debacle, all we need is one more excuse for the banks not to finance us, or for wineries to reject our grapes. There's a lot of money at stake here."

One who is willing to go on the record is Mike Porter, who manages a number of vineyards in Califor-nia's Sonoma and Napa counties. Porter, who thinks the disease is widespread, said the discussion must "come out of the closet. Nurseries, grape growers, and some plant pathologists have tried very hard to play it down. Many brooms have been kept busy trying to sweep it back under the rug, but it won't go away. It can't; it's in too many vineyards. If more people tested sick vines, they would find it. Unfortunately most sick vines are burned without testing, which is the way some nurserymen would prefer it."

Morton said she believes a majority of vineyards planted in California since 1985 are affected to some degree. "There's no way to know right now but my guess is that thirty to fifty percent of vines may be infected but may not show symptoms for some time depending on plant materials and growing conditions."

Most agree that the new disease is showing up more prominently than ever before because of more than 15,000 acres of Phylloxera-caused replantings and a general expansion of vineyard acreage in California. Napa and Sonoma farm adviser Ed Weber says, "There are more new vineyards, plus we're asking more of vines than ever before: they're being planted later in the season and have stretched the usual nursery pro-duction cycle."

In addition, most of the new vineyards in California are being planted with up to twice as many vines per acre as older vineyards. This closer proximity of vine to vine may help the pathogen spread. Finally, there is general agreement that weather—such as the California drought that ended in 1994, or floods that followed in 1995 and 1996—probably adds enough stress to help the fungus get a foothold.

Equally threatening is another old disease, one that wiped out most of the vines in Southern California's booming wine vineyards back in the 1890s. Pierce's Disease is back with a vengeance, this time in California's North Coast, where it is reaching epidemic proportions. Vineyard owners in Napa, Sonoma, Lake, and Mendocino counties say Pierce's Disease is their number one problem. There is no treatment, no cure. The only hope seems to be to genetically engineer a grapevine that is resistant to the bacteria, but with the meager research funds available, this seems a scant hope.

The bacterium that causes Pierce's Disease is present naturally in many different plants, including wild grapes, blackberries, and other plants that grow along streams and rivers. It is spread with the help of a pesky little insect called the blue-green sharpshooter, which feeds on an infected plant and then hops along into a new vineyard planted next to the woods.

The mad rush to develop more vineyards means that more land is being cleared and more vines are being planted in the sharpshooter's territory. In some ways Pierce's Disease is the ecological revenge the environment wreaks to punish the intrusion. In addition, the disease lends proof to the adage that no good deed goes unpunished. Pierce's Disease was less of a problem several years ago when growers used pesticides far more intensely than they do now. But in the past few years most growers have made a concerted effort to reduce or eliminate pesticides and rely on organic and natural farming methods instead—opening the door to the sharpshooter.

What's more, the only way for the vineyard owner to fight back is to replant the dead vine. But the replanted vine is still in the sharpshooter's own turf, it's just another good insect dining experience. Some vineyard owners have replanted three and four times over four years. Others have ripped out the vines and planted olive trees instead. Some aggressive growers are replacing the blackberries, willow trees, and other plants that host the sharpshooter with other native species: oaks, alders, redwood trees. It's expensive, but so far the only solution. Meanwhile, if you drive through California's North Coast wine country you'll see vineyards surrounded by yellow strips of what looks like crime scene tape. It's coated with a pheromone to attract the sharpshooter, both to trap and to monitor the presence of the vine assassins.

What's next for vineyard owners? Aided by a pathetic research effort, university chauvinism, industry stinginess, and the willingness to deny a problem until it is too late, the next pest is probably just right around the corner.

The lack of adequate research, and the inability of the industry to come together for the common good, aggravates the normal boom and bust cycles that characterize agriculture. An enormously devastating infestation of a new pest would be good for no one—drinkers or producers. The new devastation would reduce vineyard yields and reduce the domestic wine glut, which in turn might moderate retail wine price drops and the resulting bargains to wine consumers. It would also entail the diversion of huge financial resources toward replanting the damaged vineyards, and the resulting higher prices for wine would hurt market growth among entry-level wine drinkers who are very price sensitive.

FIVE

The Rx Files

ACCORDING TO CONSUMER RESEARCH FROM THE WINE MARket Council, the most important single factor that would prompt people to drink more wine is if they believed it was healthy for them.

Consumer uncertainty about wine and health is surprising given the conclusive, scientifically indisputable *fact* that people who drink in moderation live longer, healthier lives than either abstainers or heavy drinkers. And no matter how much bogus propaganda gets turned out by the public nags and neo-Prohibitionists, the *fact* is that this is confirmed by a vast amount of well-conducted, peer-reviewed research, respectably published in the world's most prestigious medical and scientific journals.

According to studies in *The Journal of the American*

Medical Association, The Lancet, The British Medical Journal, New England Journal of Medicine, Cardiology, and others, moderate alcohol consumption cuts cardiovascular deaths by forty to fifty percent and has a host of other beneficial effects, resisting or slowing Parkinson's and Alzheimer's disease, preserving mental acuity in the elderly, fighting macular degeneration, and helping prevent osteoporosis. Moderate consumption is generally defined as one to three glasses of wine per day for men and one or two glasses for women, because of their generally smaller body size.

Significantly, these medical and scientific studies all confirm one another, unlike many other lifestyle and health studies that often draw contradictory or equivocal conclusions (coffee is beneficial in one study, harmful in the next, and makes no difference in a third study).

The conclusive relationship between moderate alcohol consumption and longer, healthier lives is far better studied than many other medical "truths" that we take for granted. For example, the benefits of taking aspirin to prevent a heart attack rests on far shakier scientific ground than preventing heart attacks with a glass or two of wine each day.

And yet, thanks to an unrelenting stream of inaccurate, anti-alcohol disinformation on the part of those emotionally or religiously driven to support prohibition, most people and their physicians either are not aware of the overwhelming health benefits of moderate alcohol consumption or have been led to doubt the facts.

Among the worst offenders is the private Center for Science in the Public Interest, which serves as the mothership for hundreds of shrill anti-alcohol groups who are waging a holy war on demon rum (and wine and beer). These anti-alcohol groups believe, in the absence of any credible evidence, that telling the people the truth will cause a violent upsurge in drunk driving and crime.

At the federal level, this Carrie Nation mentality rules at the Department of Health and Human Services, which in the late 1980s set a goal of reducing alcohol consumption by 25 percent by the year 2000. To accomplish this, they have tried to equate alcohol consumption with AIDS, have tried to tar it with the same health-risk brush as tobacco, and have mandated that their people use the politically correct term "alcohol, tobacco, and other drugs," thus doing their level best to link a glass of Chardonnay with crack cocaine and heroin.

The government's own statistics show that alcohol abuse has not decreased. Indeed, the only people who seem susceptible to the neo-dry scare tactics are moderate and light consumers who haven't any problem with alcohol to begin with. This has resulted in a lose-lose situation for public health: the anti-alcohol fanatics have spent billions scaring away people whose health would benefit from a glass or two of wine each day, and they have wasted billions that could have been used to bring abuse treatment and prevention to those who truly needed it.

Significantly, the anti-alcohol forces spend more money each year promoting the neo-dry line than all of the advertising and promotional budgets of every American winery *combined!* Remember: the U.S. wine industry spends substantially less than $100 million each year on advertising. The federal government alone spends more than a billion dollars a year to combat "alcohol, tobacco, and other drugs." The estimate of private foundation and special interest group funds is tallied by Join Together (a privately funded anti-alcohol and other drug foundation) at more than $3 billion. Remember that the entire size of the American wine industry—from the dirt to your lips and everything in between—is only about $18 billion.

Just one special interest group—the Center for Science in the Public Interest—has an annual budget of more than $15 million, twice as large as the budgets of the Wine Institute, American Vintners Association, and every other wine industry trade organization *combined*.

This situation is unlikely to change any time soon because the wine industry lacks the resources and the will to fight the neo-drys in any effective manner. What's worse, the government has stacked the regulatory deck in favor of anti-alcohol fanatics, going so far as to prevent wineries from speaking the truth about wine and health.

Red wine sales soared in the weeks and months after the notable "60 Minutes" segment aired in November 1991, spurring anti-alcohol fanatics into action with their own inaccurate brand of spin control. The French Paradox was only for the French, they said. Actually, identical results have come from the Framingham Heart Study of Americans, among others. The anti-alcohol people then charged that the results were biased because abstainers included people who didn't drink alcohol because they were too sick. Wrong again. The studies excluded these people. Finally, the anti-alcohol folks charged that the French statistics were misleading because many French people die of cirrhosis. This was yet another smoke screen: living longer means living longer. Besides, a micro-examination of French mortality statistics show that the regions that drink the most wine have the lowest cirrhosis rates—half that of the U.S., despite the fact that people in these regions consumed more than ten times as much wine as Americans.

As false and misleading as these neo-dry pronouncements were, they were given the strength of truth by government resources and those of private anti-alcohol organizations. A politically correct bent among the nation's journalists made informing the public of the truth equally difficult.

New York Times health reporter Jane Brody was among the worst offenders. When researchers published a new story that showed moderate consumption helped prevent the common cold, she wrote in 1992: "Cigarette smoking has long been known to aggravate the common cold, but researchers were shocked to find that another common vice, alcohol, may offer some protection." Brody followed the government's lead by linking alcohol with tobacco, nor did she report that most researchers weren't shocked at all. Alcohol consumption has been shown on numerous occasions to offer protection against bacterial and viral infection (preventing hepatitis and many forms of food poisoning), so it's hardly a stretch to find it also helps protect against other forms of illness.

And where was the wine industry during all this? Mostly AWOL. The Wine Institute sat on its hands, convinced that any sort of promotion of the studies could make its members a target for product liability lawsuits, despite the fact that there might be considerable protection from such suits if there were a broad public acceptance that moderate consumption is healthy and that wine is a safe and effective product when used as directed. Former institute employees say that policy was dominated by Gallo, which profits from high-alcohol-fortified "misery wines," the equivalent of tobacco spiked with nicotine.

The Wine Institute did not want to be seen as doing absolutely nothing, so it spent a moderate amount of money making copies of medical research studies and sending them to journalists. They even bought copies of the "60 Minutes" French Paradox program and mass-mailed the videotapes to journalists who had already seen the segment. In the coming months, Wine Institute personnel would make a career of dropping little hints that they had actually been responsible for the "60 Minutes" segment, something which is simply not true.

To its credit, the Wine Institute has managed to maintain a skeleton staff of highly intelligent and dedicated people, headed by Elisabeth Holmgren in their Research and Education Department. Although chronically underfunded, Holmgren and her crew have gained wide respect for highly credible information, for sticking to the facts regarding wine and health and not overstating the benefits. However, at its height, before the drastic budget cuts of the mid 1990s, the Wine Institute never devoted more than $500,000 in any given year to the health issue, the single most important issue affecting consumer decisions. Of that half-million dollars, no more than $120,000 ever actually funded research; the rest went to institute salaries, travel, and other activities. This is, of course, just a fraction of a drop in a huge bucket when contrasted with the billions spent on propaganda to convince people that all alcohol consumption is bad.

Of course, a small but credible amount of research

has been done and published without the institute's involvement. But ironically, each published study gets less and less attention than the ones that preceded it because they all reach the same conclusions: if you are part of the 93 percent of adults who can drink without abusing, you'll live a longer, healthier life if you drink moderately—don't drink too much, but don't abstain. And meanwhile, the Wine Institute's reluctance to take up the French Paradox as an issue helped it lose even more members. In 1991, Robert Mondavi cited it as the final straw that resulted in its resignation from that organization. Scores of smaller wineries followed suit for the same or similar reasons.

The experience of one of those smaller wineries, Leeward Winery near Santa Barbara, illustrates the level of frustration on the part of wineries trying to spur action from the Wine Institute, and a feeling by the wineries of what can only be called betrayal. On March 30, 1992, the five-person, 12,000-case winery mailed 1,800 copies of its newsletter containing an article that quoted from the "60 Minutes" program on the French Paradox. Less than a week later the Bureau of Alcohol, Tobacco and Firearms threatened Leeward with the loss of its license to do business. The BATF said that it had determined that the newsletter was in fact an advertisement and that it was strictly forbidden to make any mention of beneficial health effects in an advertisement, no matter how factual the ad was.

Leeward asked the Wine Institute for help. After all, it was a member of the institute and had listened for years to the rhetoric about how powerful the institute was and how sharp its legal experts were and how well it looked after smaller wineries, despite being funded by Gallo and the big boys. Chuck Brigham, one of Leeward's owners, told me: "We asked for the Wine Institute's help, but they pretty much sidestepped."

Leeward resigned from the Wine Institute and found instead John Hinman, a San Francisco attorney whose firm specializes in alcoholic beverage law. Few people love a fight more than Hinman, especially when it involves the BATF against the underdog he found in Leeward. Hinman and his partner, Lynne Carmichael, were closely allied with the Family Winemakers of California, and thus had little but disdain for the Wine Institute's lack of action.

Because of Leeward's small size and the wine industry's usual failure to contribute to causes that advance its own self interest, Hinman's fight on behalf of Leeward was more pro bono than profitable. Hinman and his partners fought the BATF to a standstill in the Leeward case. Hinman's efforts grew into a loosely governed organization called the Coalition for Truth and Balance, whose goal became the development of a government-approved, scientifically reviewed and factually balanced statement regarding the French Paradox that wineries could use without fear of the BATF's hit men showing up at their doors ready to shred business permits. Characteristically, the Wine Institute refused to cooperate with Hinman and his clients on the preparation of what became a 664-word statement that contained so many scientific references and footnotes that no stretch of any rational imagination could construe it as an attempt to sell wine as medicine. (The statement is reproduced as Appendix C.)

In the months after the BATF kicked in Leeward's First Amendment doors, they went into full book-burning mode to keep Domain Chandon, Robert Mondavi, and other wineries from mentioning the "60 Minutes" program on the French Paradox in winery newsletters, or in any other manner. The BATF even went after an advertising supplement in the *New York Times* that contained references to the French Paradox, and went after a series of newspaper advertisements paid for by the French trade organization, Food and Wines from France.

Another European winemaker had a similarly inexcusable confrontation with the BATF. On a fine Sausalito day, May 27, 1992, the dark suits from the BATF showed up at Miramar Torres's door demanding to know the details about her brother's quote in the *Washington Post* that day in which he said (with a reasonable amount of scientific backing) that in his opinion wine was more inherently healthy than cow's milk. Miramar, who runs the Torres family's North American operation (her brother runs the family business in Spain), and her executives were terrified that they would be put out of business by the BATF's storm trooper actions. "This was outrageous," Miramar told me. "We can't let them continue to get away with this kind of censorship." But get away with it they did—and continue to do—simply because no one in the business needs the hassles.

One can see the roots of the federal government's prejudice against alcohol when viewed against the mandate placing the regulation of wine alongside that of machine guns, bombs, and cancer-causing tobacco products, which are inherently unsafe when consumed as recommended. And when you give a neo-Prohibitionist the power to put someone out of the wine business for speaking the truth, you have created a very effective gag on their freedom of speech.

The petty irrationality of the BATF even extended to threatening San Francisco wine retailer Jerome

Draper with revocation of his license in 1993 because he was giving away red heart-shaped buttons with the words, "Have You Had Your Wine Today?" The BATF justified its threat against Draper by citing a long-standing policy against therapeutic claims for alcohol that was developed in response to patent medicines: "While this regulatory prohibition only applies to untrue or misleading statements, in practice we hold that *all therapeutic claims, regardless of their truthfulness, to be inherently misleading and particularly deceptive* [italics mine] in view of the possible social effect of encouraging the consumption of alcoholic beverages." The BATF rationalized this position by explaining that because Congress had mandated warning labels on all alcoholic beverages, to juxtapose something positive about alcohol—no matter how true—would be misleading!

Significantly, the Wine Institute did nothing during this period to assist the wineries under assault by the BATF, nor to fight for their First Amendment rights to speak the truth about the French Paradox. Indeed, an entirely separate case, *44 Liquor Mart v. Rhode Island*, involving a liquor retailer's right to advertise prices, which came before the U.S. Supreme Court in 1996, finally resulted in constitutional protection for the sort of information that Leeward Winery and others had tried to print. Rhode Island's law was supposed to keep alcohol consumption down by preventing competition among retailers that could result in lower prices.

In this case, the U.S. Supreme Court said that it was unconstitutional, calling the law "paternalistic" and stating: "Precisely because bans against truthful, non-misleading commercial speech rarely seek to protect consumers from either deception or overreaching, they usually rest solely on the offensive assumption that the public will respond 'irrationally' to the truth. The First Amendment directs us to be especially skeptical of regulations that seek to keep people in the dark for what the government perceives to be their own good. That teaching applies equally to state attempts to deprive consumers of accurate information about their chosen products." The Supreme Court decision noted that "evidence suggests that the abusive drinker will probably not be deterred by a marginal price increase and that the true alcoholic may simply reduce his purchase of other necessities." Instead of trying to throttle the truth, the Supreme Court said the preferable alternative is to assume that "people will perceive their own best interests if only they are well enough informed, and that the means to that end is to open the channels of communication rather than to close them."

"Once again—as with CBS's "60 Minutes"—the wine industry has benefited accidentally from the hard work of others rather than rolling up its sleeves and fighting its own battles.

On numerous occasions, Wine Institute president John DeLuca told me he felt that Hinman's efforts on behalf of Leeward and similar clients were "irresponsible." "I knew the biggest threat to us was if the legal community was set loose on us, like tobacco or asbestos," DeLuca told a reporter for my magazine, *Wine Business Monthly*, in March 1994. "I had wineries that wanted to sell wine almost like a health food and I said that was very dangerous."

DeLuca explained that he felt the alternate path he had chosen—encouraging research while lobbying the government—was a better, safer way. The Wine Institute's lobbying—along with that from the Coalition for Truth and Balance and the Competitive Enterprise Institute—did seem to contribute to a softening of the federal government's rabid anti-alcohol stance, as reflected in a 1995 revision of the U.S. Dietary guidelines in which the government dropped the statements that alcohol consumption "was not recommended" and had "no health benefits." The guidelines now state that alcohol is best consumed with meals and is "associated with a lower risk of coronary artery disease."

Then, reversing its earlier stance that any sort of reference to the French Paradox on wine bottles was dangerous, in mid-1996 the Wine Institute submitted to the BATF a label referring consumers to the Dietary Guidelines. The label joined one already submitted nine months earlier by the Coalition for Truth and Balance, which read: "The proud people who made this wine encourage you to consult with your family doctor about the health benefits and risks of moderate wine consumption."

This approach, however, has the same potential for failure as the Wine Institute's emphasis on developing more and more research that is read less and less. False and misleading statements spread by anti-alcohol forces and their nearly unlimited budgets assure it. Contrary to the scientific proof, they say the benefits of moderate consumption are slight (the evidence suggests a forty to fifty percent reduction in deaths from cardiovascular disease), moderate consumers don't live longer (they do by an average of about two years), moderate consumption leads to abuse (false), increases in liver disease and cancer outweigh the benefits (false), and so on. Just enough doubt has been cast on the scientific results for reasonable people to disbelieve them. One more study or an additional ream of research added to the overwhelmingly conclusive evidence so far developed won't make any difference so long as the wine industry remains silent.

Shamefully, this ignorance of the scientific and medical facts extends to many family physicians, despite the Coalition for Truth and Balance's desire to rely upon them. When Dr. Keith Marton, an assistant professor of medicine at the University of California, San Francisco Medical School, and then head of the Department of Medicine at the California Pacific Medical Center, polled a group of visiting physicians in 1995, he found that almost three-quarters of the doctors were unaware of the substantial benefits of moderate alcohol consumption and the extent to which those benefits had been conclusively proven. A nationwide poll in 1994 by the American Wine Alliance for Research and Education (AWARE) found that 47 percent of physicians were unaware that moderate consumption decreased the risk of heart disease. To be sure, the physicians involved had shirked their professional obligations to remain current on medical research. But it's equally obvious that the anti-alcohol misinformation has gone a long way toward keeping most doctors from writing a prescription for a glass of wine, to be consumed slowly and with food.

So, as the wine industry slouches toward a new millennium, the government and the anti-alcohol fanatics that support it will continue to deny everything that is scientifically supportable. The wine industry's lack of will means that the real medical truth about moderate consumption will remain obscured, leaving consumers unaware of the truth—a truth that could prolong or even save their lives.

Health information is the most important single issue affecting wine consumption in the United States.

If the industry continues to remain silent, it will keep consumption from rising at more than nominal levels. But if the neo-Prohibitionists mount a strong campaign that is unanswered by the industry, then consumption is likely to begin falling, aggravating the coming wine glut and further depressing retail wine prices. Again, good for buying wine, and not so good for buying a winery, vineyard, or their stock.

SIX

Relics of Prohibition

IT'S EVERY PARENT'S NIGHTMARE: COMING HOME FROM DINner early to find the tranquillity of the evening split asunder by the shrieks of uncontrolled sipping, swirling, and spitting, the front lawn littered with the empties of $50 Cabernets surreptitiously ordered with Dad's credit card from an Internet cyberbootlegger.

"Teens with Taste" might be a frightening thought to parents, but you would be hard pressed to find a parent or any other rational person who thinks that millions of teens are scheming right now to sneak away one of their parents' credit cards, order a $400 case of Cabernet, wait two or three weeks and then go on a bender. But not the Attorney General of New York, and like-minded cronies in Kentucky, Georgia, and other states. They're working with a gang of liquor wholesalers and distributors to create one fiction after another in a desperately greedy attempt to protect a patchwork of anticonsumer monopolies that do little more than line their own pockets at your expense.

These are the folks who are against direct shipping of wine. They're also the reason why you can't buy most of the wines made by most small wineries in America. If you live in New York state or its political bedfellows on this issue—Arkansas, Florida, Georgia, Kentucky, Mississippi, Maine, North Dakota, Tennessee, or Utah—you're the patsy of a monopolistic cartel-like system that gives middlemen carte blanche to jack up wine prices all they want. This anticompetitive system deprives you of a wide range of wine choices that can only be found (at lower prices) in the twelve so-called reciprocal states: California, Colorado, Idaho, Illinois, Missouri, Minnesota, Missouri, Nebraska, New Mexico, Oregon, Washington, and West Virginia. These states have acted in their citizens' interest rather than those of the middlemen who have bought the influence of their politicians with millions of dollars in campaign contributions.

To understand the problem, you need to understand how wine gets to you. Its distribution system is made up of three tiers: producer, wholesaler/distributor, and retailer. There are different classes of licenses for each of these tiers, and in general it is illegal for a single person or business entity to hold all three classes of license. The sole exception is California, where people who agree to sell wine only—no beer or spirits—can sell on all three tiers.

The three-tier system was instituted at the end of Prohibition. The theory behind it, which has worked about as well as the theory behind Prohibition itself, is that stopping any company from being vertically integrated would help keep out organized crime and help prevent monopolies.

The system never kept criminals out of the business, it just kept their ownership at arm's length. In practice, the regulations, enforced by the BATF, are just a minor annoyance to convicted felons and organized crime. And the system certainly has not prevented the rise of monopolies.

Once, the three-tier system served the marketplace well. For years, distributors had salespeople on their payrolls who knew their local customers and markets, knew their products, and worked hard to represent the brands. Wine salespeople tasted the wine, knew the wineries, and could become real advocates for the wines they sold. In general, beer and spirits salespeople stuck to their beverages and wine salespeople sold only wine, because the latter took a lot more knowledge to sell. In most cases, however, wine salespeople were looked down upon because profit margins are generally smaller than for beer and spirits. So, if two reps sold the same dollar amount in a given month, the beer/wine salesperson was more valued by the distributor for contributing more profit.

The distributor/wholesaler made it possible for the winery, brewer, or distillery to maintain a smaller sales force. The system also worked well for restaurants and retail outlets, which now had a marketing partner long before that phrase became a B-school buzzword.

Thirty or forty years ago, the system looked like an inverted funnel, with producers at the top, a larger number of distributors in the middle, a much larger number of restaurants and retail outlets below that, and consumers at the very base. In 1963 the BATF listed more than 10,900 wholesale permits and 377 wine producers in the United States; many wholesaler/distributors carried no wine brands at all. Even counting import brands, each wholesaler carried few enough brands so that each brand could be represented fairly by the salespeople. There were a fair number of "fine wine only" wholesalers run by people in love with wine, who hired salespeople of like mind.

But since then the system has changed for the worse. By 1997 the number of wholesalers had shrunk to less than 3,000—a 70 percent attrition rate. What's worse for wine is that just 25 of those control almost 60 percent of the market. But over the same period of time, the number of American wine producers has exploded to almost 1,800.

So the system that once looked like an inverted funnel is today shaped more like an hourglass. Wholesalers who once sold and facilitated the sales of wine are now choke points, order takers who have lost the skills to actually sell their products. Those wholesalers represent so many different wine brands that only a handful from the very largest and most profitable wineries get any attention at all.

According to the Gomberg-Fredrikson Report, an industry statistical mainstay, 97 percent of all the wine exported from California (to other states or abroad) comes from 68 wineries (out of a state total of about 750). These are obviously the big, profitable brands that a wholesaler in Florida or New York or Kentucky would spend the most time selling. Not only do these brands offer higher profit margins, they tend to be better known to—and purchased by—the average consumer.

What about the other three percent of the wine

made by the remaining wineries, half of which sell less than 3,000 cases (36,000 bottles) of wine every year? The answer is obvious. Most can't get a distributor to carry them. And those *un*lucky enough to be picked up by one of the giants such as Southern Wines and Spirits (the industry leader with an 11 percent U.S. market share and annual sales of more than $2.4 billion) languish, buried at the bottom of a list that grows ever larger as the middle tier continues to consolidate.

Most of these small wineries, and hundreds more like them in Oregon, Washington, New York, Ohio, Virginia, Maryland, Missouri, and 39 other U.S. states where wine is made, are small, family-owned operations with marginal finances. As with any other business, increased sales is the fastest route to a sounder balance sheet.

The same is true, however, for the retailer, who needs to stock wines that move off the shelves quickly. There is a limited amount of shelf space even in the largest stores. California's Beverages and more!, for example, has brought the Borders/Costco superstore approach to wine, beer, and spirits. But even here, shelves are carefully arranged, employing computer software that uses scanner sales data along with prices and profit margins to draw a schematic of the shelves and tell the stocking clerks exactly where to put specific bottles and how many of them to display. No matter how much shelf space, inventory is a drag if it doesn't turn over quickly.

One solution for small wineries is to sell directly to consumers who have learned about these boutique wines from a visit to the winery, a taste in a restaurant or with friends, or through wine clubs, the Internet, or other sources. The same holds true for small microbreweries.

Because of this importance, the Wine Institute—in what ranks as their most valuable service to small winery members—has helped negotiate a number of reciprocal agreements with other states in which direct shipment is allowed.

There used to be thirteen reciprocal states, but Maine legislators acted quickly to repeal that agreement when the distributors pulled the strings attached to their campaign contributions. In August 1995, the New York legislature agreed to join the reciprocal states' club, but distributors leaned hard on Gov. George Pataki, who caved in and vetoed the bill. New York has been particularly victimized by the middle of the three-tier system, with wholesalers almost succeeding (also in 1995) in repealing newly passed legislation allowing wine auctions in that state.

It is clear that these monopolists in every state are a lot like mobsters operating a protection racket: they don't want a single bottle of wine sold without getting a cut from it, even if they did nothing at all to earn the money.

As a result, small wineries and microbreweries are twisting slowly in the wind as the three-tier system and the cartels that profit from its fossilized remains block direct shipping and try to repeal reciprocal agreements in the remaining states. Not satisfied with almost a hundred percent of the markets, the distributors—led by Southern Wines and Spirits—have done their best to keep consumers from buying directly from the wineries. Beginning in 1995, the distributors called in the IOUs from their hefty campaign contributions, and in record time convinced the legislatures in Georgia, Kentucky, North Carolina, Florida, and other states to make direct shipping a felony. They went even further, pressuring the attorneys general in New York and other states to intercept and seize shipments of wine sent from California wineries to consumers in their states. For many small wineries and microbreweries, the direct shipments are the difference between success and bankruptcy.

"Amazingly, the wholesalers knew what they were doing to us," said Matanzas Creek Winery's Bill Mac-Iver, who co-founded the Coalition for Free Trade to battle restrictions on direct shipping. "They just didn't give a damn. When it was pointed out that the mandatory three-tier system could drive small wineries out of business if enforced, one mighty distributor in one of our most important markets said, 'Tough luck.' "

The crackdown on direct shipping began in earnest in December 1994 with several large consolidated wine shipments being seized in New Jersey and Maryland. The seizures capped off a year of escalating resistance to direct shipping that included threats of legal action and fines from Michigan, Massachusetts, and Texas.

One of the greatest threats in the late 1990s was a legal assault against direct shipping in Florida following a steady series of complaints from executives at megadistributor Southern Wine and Spirits, which convinced Florida to ask for help from the BATF. What frustrated Southern executives and the Florida law enforcement officials who were in bed with them was the lack of a clearly defined way to strike back at the wineries whose wines were getting into consumers' hands without Southern getting its cut from the sale. Florida tax authorities professed to be concerned about the loss of tax revenues, but later moderated their tone when it was pointed out that the actual lost revenues were not large enough to justify an all-out assault. Florida was also vulnerable on another card that the wine industry never played: violation of equal protection under the law. The volume of taxes lost to Florida from Land's End, L.L.Bean, and other catalogue merchants of non-alcohol-related products is thousands of times greater, yet efforts to recover those taxes never reached the irrational intensity leveled at directly shipped wines.

The enforcement problems began with the repeal of Prohibition, accompanied by a piece of "enabling legislation" called the Webb-Kenyon Act. The act gives each state the legal right to regulate alcohol any way it chooses, even to restrict interstate commerce, which would otherwise be unconstitutional. What is left is statutory chaos: fifty-one different sets of regulations (each state plus federal); different licensing requirements for producers (federal), wholesaler/distributors (federal and state), and retailers (state). It all adds up to fifty-one fabulously fat bureaucracies—headaches and needless paperwork for the businesses involved, higher prices for consumers, government-sanctioned monopolies for distributors, and a full-employment plan for attorneys.

Florida officials felt that Webb-Kenyon gave them the right to fine wineries and retailers and wine clubs that shipped directly into the state. But as state law enforcement officials, they did not have direct jurisdiction over the wineries. Prodded into action by Southern Wine and Spirits, Florida upped the ante and in December 1994 convinced the BATF to formulate a policy that said a winery could lose its basic permit (the one allowing it to make wine) for any violations of the Webb-Kenyon Act. The BATF reiterated its stand that it had no control over retailers, wine clubs, or other nonproducers because federal law did not govern them. Wine Country Congressman Frank Riggs and other legislators representing California, Oregon, and Washington state went into action and forced the BATF to put its threats on the back burner, where they reside today. Undeterred, the Wine and Spirits Wholesalers of America and other wholesaler special interest groups lobbied for an amendment to Webb-Kenyon that would have provided for federal penalties for nonproducers. In an unaccustomed fit of sanity, Congress let that bill die in 1997. It will, however, probably be revived as wholesalers continue to lose their battle for unearned income.

But back in November 1995, stung by the BATF's inability to step in and solve the problem for them, Florida filed suit in federal district court against seven direct shippers: Zachy's Wine and Liquor and Rochambeau Wines and Liquors, both of New York, and five California companies—the California Wine Club, St. Helena Wine Merchants, Passport Wine Club, Stafford's Fine Wine and Specialty Co., and the Wine Club of Santa Ana. State officials demanded the payment of millions of dollars in fines, fees, and unpaid taxes, and asked the federal court to compel the BATF to take action against the wineries whose wine was being shipped.

As the case came to trial in May 1996, Florida received a major embarrassment when court documents revealed that its case was built around a "sting" conducted by none other than Southern Wine and Spirits. The prosecution's documentation was based on wine ordered from out of state by company officials who placed "illegal" orders so that there would be an offense to prosecute. The judge threw out the case, arguing that a federal court had no authority to enforce a state tax law nor did it have the authority to compel the BATF to act against wineries. Predictably, Southern, through its Florida state surrogates, appealed, shopping it to a state court where they presumed they would get a better hearing.

But no sooner had the appeal been filed than one of the key figures in the case rebelled. In a bizarre turn of events, Florida Attorney General Bob Butterworth asked for a postponement of the trial so he could submit a proposed bill to the legislature that offered a compromise worked out with the Coalition for Free Trade. Butterworth got the postponement and submitted a bill that would have legalized direct shipping through a tax collection program requiring shippers to be licensed by the state and pay the appropriate taxes.

Any remaining doubt that the tax issue was a straw dog manufactured to cover up the real motive evaporated when the Florida wholesalers jerked on the strings that connected campaign contributions to legislators. Thanks to wholesaler opposition, Attorney General Butterworth's rational compromise plan was dead before the ink had dried. Not only did the legislature fail to consider a bill that clearly addressed every issue that had been raised, but in the words of CFT's MacIver, "Just to show Florida's top law enforcement officer who was really boss, the wholesalers' lobby immediately forced through a bill that made direct shipping a felony instead of a misdemeanor." Instead of simply paying a fine for direct shipping, a winery could face the revocation of its basic permit.

Attorney General Butterworth wrote to Gov. Lawton Chiles urging him to veto the bill: "Florida simply does not need to criminalize businesses and citizens in order to deal with the profound changes occurring in the highly competitive global marketplace, changes that offer Florida consumers greater variety and better prices than they have ever known before." He called the felony measure "an unnecessary and counterproductive measure that will hurt Florida consumers as well as our state's reputation nationally." Wholesalers, Butterworth wrote, "have a vise grip on the distribution of alcoholic beverages" and they "cling stubbornly to the outmoded ways of the past, refusing to accommodate the realities of the modern marketplace." The felony bill "harms so many people, only to benefit a small group of individuals who control Florida's alcoholic beverage industry."

Gov. Chiles approved the felony bill in late May 1997.

Boycott talk surfaced immediately. More than sixty California wineries, including giant Kendall-Jackson, had been boycotting Kentucky for more than a year following that state's approval of felony penalties for direct shipping. Now the talk turned toward urging the California governor and legislature to boycott Florida orange juice—or even to make it a felony to ship Florida orange juice into California.

Meanwhile, as the summer of 1997 rolled by, things looked bleaker for small wineries. Maine repealed its reciprocity law, North Carolina made direct shipping a felony, and the American Vintners Association caused additional rifts within the organization by holding its annual meeting in Georgia despite that state's passage of a felony direct shipping law. The battle continued in the courts, with the BATF filing in the U.S. Eleventh Circuit Court of Appeals for jurisdiction in the issue.

As the fall approached, winery and wholesaler organizations held several meetings that produced no results because the wholesalers felt fat, happy, and on top.

But the tide began to shift in Florida when a state court threw the wholesalers' case out. Presumably, the wholesalers had overlooked this judge on their campaign Christmas list. Then, on October 24, 1997, the Eleventh Circuit Court of Appeals unanimously ruled that states have no right to ask federal courts or officials to enforce state laws. The U.S. Supreme Court affirmed the decision in May 1998.

The integrity of the Florida Attorney General's office unfortunately does not extend to the state of New York, where A.G. Dennis Vacco allowed himself to be a willing tool for the wholesalers' newest poster issue: children.

With the good taste and restraint of antibeef protesters throwing bloody cattle guts on a packing plant manager, the wholesalers set up a sham organization, Americans for Responsible Alcohol Access (ARAA), wholly funded by the Wine and Spirits Wholesalers of America, which plastered the news media with releases that charged that "Internet booze merchants" were selling directly to children and delivering to their homes. There had never been a complaint from a parent or local official in any state, and there was no evidence that teens seeking to get drunk would willingly spend the money for premium wines and then wait two weeks to get a tasteful buzz.

"We charge $27 for two six-packs of beer," said Jim Lowe of Hogshead Beer Cellars, a microbrew-of-the-month club in Greensboro, North Carolina. "If an eighteen-year-old's got $27 burning a hole in his pocket, he's going to give it to an older brother to buy three or four cases of cheap beer . . . and they're certainly not going to do what we require: wait for it."

Every U.S. government study conducted supports the direct shippers' contentions, noting that beer—cheap and locally obtained—is the number one beverage of abuse for underage drinkers, followed by sweet coolers, vodka and fruit juices, and soft drinks laced with spirits such as rum or bourbon.

In the unlikely event that teens with taste did "borrow" one of their parents' credit cards and order illicit microbrews or Chardonnay, they would have to remain at home almost all day, every day, for two weeks, waiting for the package to arrive in order to hide it from Mom and Dad. Then there is the day of reckoning when the credit card bill arrives with the charge duly noted. Any teenager dumb enough not to recognize that the bill is going to nab them is probably also too clueless to avoid the direct shippers' safeguards in the first place.

Yet Vacco pressed ahead. In the moderate, measured words of the wholesalers' press release: "First it was cyberporn . . . now it's cyberbooze." To prove their point, they carefully coached a dozen teenagers on how to evade safeguards against selling or shipping to underage people to entrap eleven direct shippers.

The wholesalers produced a video for Vacco on the "dramatic sting," as they called it. Most journalists saw through Vacco's staged publicity skit and saw the wholesalers behind it.

After all of the sound bites about protecting children, Vacco's list of companies did not include one single New York State direct shipper—despite the fact that those shippers legally send tens of thousands of shipments of wine to state residents, in precisely the same manner, with the same safeguards. If direct shipping doesn't pose a problem to children when it comes from New York State shippers, it certainly can't pose a problem when done in exactly the same way by out-of-state businesses.

And after defaming these businesses before the press and charging them with heinous crimes against children, Vacco never filed charges against any of the companies he named in his media sideshow. He claims he still intends to press for a felony direct shipping provision in New York, but the staged falsity of the stunt, reminiscent as it was of old-time Soviet or Cuban propaganda, seems to have cost Vacco and the wholesalers' credibility. And the fact that the New York legislature would press for legislation against newspaper and magazine advertisements, which is clearly unconstitutional even to a first-year law student, seems to be firm evidence that distributor money speaks louder than the Bill of Rights. It may also have cost Vacco credibility with voters who kicked him out of office in 1998.

The wholesalers' stunt also helped advance the cause of the neo-Prohibitionist movement, which wants to see alcohol consumption decrease dramatically without regard to whether it is delivered directly or through the three-tier system. As one prominent neo-dry group, Join Together, put it: "Direct shipping undoes the entire fabric of our social policy on alcohol control."

Wholesalers recognize that the products they distribute account for most of the alcohol abuse in America— underage or not. And like the Hamas bomber who straps the explosives under his armpits and walks into the local café, the large wholesalers seem willing to destroy themselves rather than cede even a bit of legitimacy to people who don't pay them their per-bottle protection fee. The irony of the situation is that—words of protest aside—wholesalers have demonstrated by their failure to represent small brands that they cannot, will not, and do not care to handle the sorts of wines and micro-brews that are being shipped directly.

Lost in all this flying fur is the American Vintners Association's stillborn solution, Cellarmasters of America, which exists on a sub-respirator level with a handful of wineries that no one has ever heard of. The system concocted by Cellarmasters was doomed to failure even before it started: it was too expensive, required wineries to cede many of their distribution and representation rights, and consisted of a Rube Goldbergian system that makes the Webb-Kenyon Act look positively linear.

The Cellarmasters' failure, the wholesaler losses in court, Vacco's freak show, and certainly some new surprises waiting to be sprung as this book is being written, mean that there are many cards remaining to be played out in this game. Unfortunately, the battle is between small shippers and the consumers they serve, and an entrenched, well-financed wholesalers' cartel whose money reaches into the pockets of legislators and public officials in every state and in the nation's capital.

The outcome will most certainly affect your choices of wines and the prices you pay.

SEVEN

Counterfeit Wines: Fakes, Frauds, and the Merely Deceptive

Y OU CAN'T ALWAYS JUDGE A WINE BY ITS LABEL.

You may be merely misled by labels and ads that are cleverly worded to make it seem that you're getting a more prestigious wine than is actually in the bottle. In the worst of cases, ranging from fake Burgundies to counterfeit champagnes, what comes out of the bottle may be something entirely different from what the label claims.

In both cases, the deceit takes your wallet for a bumpy ride.

And as with the counterfeiting of currency, designer watches, or software, deception peaks with prices and shortages. When an item is valuable, expensive, or scarce enough, then it's worth the risk of getting caught. Wine is no different in this manner from Nike sneakers or Gucci handbags.

Most often, the fraud goes undetected because (1) there are no reliable methods for checking wines once they are in the bottle, and (2) most very expensive wines are bought by people who can't tell the difference between merely good wine and great wine and/or have purchased the bottle not so much for the taste but as a status symbol. Experts who sample one of the fakes will sometimes chalk up an inferior taste to "travel shock," bad storage conditions, or the catchall phrase covering so many sins that it has become meaningless: "bottle variation." The fact that so many experts somehow feel obligated to make excuses for highly touted bottles that fail to measure up is a license for the unscrupulous to shove fake wine into the marketplace. The reality is that many fanatically touted and overpriced wines are simply overrated, and the impostor wine in the bottle happens to be better than the plonk that the winery on the label can bottle by itself. This is a dirty little secret that wineries and wine writers must protect because their economic lives depend on it. The irrational worship of some highly acclaimed wines is a mostly artificial creation of wine writers and wine geeks so they can argue about the meaningless decision of what is the greatest wine in the world. In reality, most of this is marketing hype. For every $400 per bottle Burgundy (or $100 California Cabernet), you can find one costing a quarter as much that is equally as good, but just doesn't happen to lie within an outdated set of geographic boundaries.

One of the grandest international conspiracies to produce counterfeit wine combined French greed with Panamanian corruption, the Cuban government's desperate need for hard currency, and the likely collusion of the South African national wine cooperative.

In 1987, Charley Delmare, a senior lecturer with the respected international wine governing and standards organization, Office Internationale du Vin, and a co-conspirator, Jean-Claude Remaury, a well-known French winemaking consultant, signed a deal with the Castro government to make wine coolers at the old national rum distillery, forty miles from Havana. The plans were to make the coolers, affix counterfeit labels of top U.S. brands, launder them through Panamanian warehouses owned by then-dictator Manuel Noriega's son-in-law, and ship them into the United States, where they would be moved through importers and wholesalers involved in the scheme.

The cooler project was abandoned less than a year later because profit margins were so slim, competition was too tough in the U.S., and the volume of liquid to be shipped was so large. In addition, the cooler market was an almost entirely American phenomenon, which meant that the wily counterfeiters had no alternative market. This was particularly important because even the crooked importer/wholesalers in the United States were afraid to cross E. & J. Gallo, whose Bartles & Jaymes cooler was the leading brand ("Thank you for your support"), and whose salespeople are known for taking no prisoners.

Looking for a higher-profit item that could be sold worldwide, Delmare and Remaury settled on something they both knew very well: French Champagne. Specifically, they targeted Moët et Chandon Brut Imperial because it retailed for $40 to $50 per bottle in the U.S. and had a high enough production volume so that a few hundred thousand additional bottles would not be noticed, especially in America, where palates, they reasoned, were not as discriminating.

They set to work with Delmare using his connections to obtain bottles, corks, and foil capsules identical to those used by Moët. Remaury was the wine consultant in charge of obtaining the stuff that was to be bottled.

The scheme was very attractive to the Cuban government, its economy staggering from the American trade embargo, and with a Russian government no longer willing or able to prop up the doddering Communist regime. "It was one of Castro's schemes to make hard currency," one of the French investigators told me. "And what better source than from his old adversary, the USA? He has learned much about counterfeiting from his Communist allies in China. It is a problem for well-known French brands." China is known for ripping off everything from Louis Vuitton handbags and Rolex watches to Hermès scarves and Windows 95.

French investigators said they believe the counterfeit Moët was shipped through the ports of New Orleans and Miami and "distributed and sold in Atlanta and Dallas, where they probably wouldn't know the difference." And they were right. In fact, the scheme might never have unraveled had not the United States decided to invade Panama. Tipped off by Castro that an American invasion of Panama was certain, the counterfeiters in September 1989 shipped the remaining stock of fake Moët to France and sold it to a French company, Ixel de Vannes (West), which tipped off French authorities following a rash of complaints about the taste.

The pair were arrested in 1991 along with a third man, Marc Proux-Delrouyre, who was stabbed to death shortly afterward in a crime that remains unsolved.

Delrouyre's role in the scam is unclear, but he may have been the primary liaison with the South Africans.

The Paris Criminal Court convicted Delmare and Remaury in April 1992 and fined them almost $1 million. The men also received suspended prison sentences for having shipped 120,000 bottles (10,000 cases) of the fake Moët into France. French investigators said they thought at least twice that amount had been sold in the United States. The trail might have ended there, but in June 1997 the *Mail & Guardian*, a newspaper in Capetown, South Africa, published an extensive investigative article accusing the national wine cooperative, KWV, of longtime collusion in Champagne fraud schemes dating from the same time that Delmare and Remaury were setting up shop in Cuba. Indeed, the *Mail & Guardian* reported: "In 1993 there was more hard evidence of South African involvement in a champagne swindle when police seized 900,000 fake Moët et Chandon and Dom Pérignon labels which had been printed in Stellenbosch [a prime South African wine region] and were awaiting shipment to Panama." The *Mail & Guardian* reported further that "during their investigations, the police seized documents showing KWV had exported nearly one million liters of Chenin Blanc and Colombard wines to Cuba in 1990 which had been ordered by 'two foreigners.' "

The "two foreigners" were almost without doubt Delmare and Remaury. Chenin Blanc and Colombard (known in the United States as "French Colombard") have long been vinted into sparkling wines vaguely resembling Champagne. They are cheaper grapes, costing about one-fifth as much as Pinot Noir and other traditional grapes used in making real Champagne.

The main Champagne fraud on which the *Mail &*

Guardian's article concentrated involved the fabrication of two bogus brands: "Paul Lambert" and "Charles Lemond." The *Mail & Guardian* obtained KMV documents indicating that the Lambert and Lemond faux-Champagnes were "made with South African wines and bottled in South Africa with counterfeit labels complete with fake French coding." French authorities confirmed that neither brand exists in France. What is known is that the wines were shipped to the United States and were being sold in 1991 for about $5 per bottle.

Burgundy wines, both red and white, are probably the world's most counterfeited and adulterated wines. Some reds, like Domaine Romanée-Conti, can sell for hundreds of dollars per bottle, and very limited production from prized vineyards which are frequently less than ten acres create the profit incentives.

Winemaking fraud is endemic in Burgundy despite efforts of the government and a few winemakers to clean up the region's act. Because of antiquated, needlessly complicated, and frequently flawed regulations, one vineyard may be designated a grand cru while an equally good one a stone's throw away might receive a lower village rating, its grapes and the resulting wines fetching perhaps a quarter of the neighbor's price. This situation is complicated by the insatiable worldwide thirst for Burgundy wines. So it should be no surprise that appellation fraud is a way of life in Burgundy and tends to be winked at by the Burgundians and French authorities alike.

The most common Burgundian grape fraud involves purchasing cheap Gamay grapes from Beaujolais to stretch the limited amount of Burgundian fruit available. In addition, large quantities of wine are shipped in by large tanker trucks from the Rhône Valley, most commonly the Châteauneuf-du-Pape region. Regional lore tells of vintners trying to sneak tanker trucks in during the night only to stumble over neighbors doing the same thing.

In addition to grape fraud, an even more common deceit in Burgundy is the simultaneous chaptalization and acidification of wines.

Chaptalization is the addition of sugar to grape must (crushed but unfermented grape juice and skins) when the grapes come in from the vineyard with a sugar level too low to reach minimum levels, about 12 percent alcohol by volume. The alcohol in wine comes, of course, from the fermentation of the sugar. Sugar levels in grapes are known as brix, and in general there is a brix-to-alcohol conversion of about 55 percent, give or take a percent or two depending on myriad conditions. Thus, grapes harvested with a brix of 22 would produce a wine with about 12 percent alcohol. Alcohol not only adds a "mouth feel" and buzz to wine, it plays a key role in extracting flavors from the skins and in preserving the wine so it will not spoil.

But a growing season that is too cool, too cloudy, or too short can produce grape sugar levels too low to make good wine. In most of the world, adding sugar is looked upon as adulteration, but in Burgundy the law allows chaptalization that boosts alcohol levels by up to two percent. But when there is a vintage at stake and bills to pay, most Burgundian winemakers don't stop at two percent.

Unfortunately, the sorts of conditions that result in low grape sugar also produce low acid levels, a problem that can be aggravated by the use of certain agricultural chemicals. When this happens, wineries are tempted to boost the acid levels artificially. Drinkers experience acid as tartness or as a balance against the sugar levels. Simultaneous chaptalization and acidification has been illegal in France since 1913, and in 1987 was made part of the winemaking laws of the European Union. One outspoken Frenchman, journalist Michel Bettane of *La Revue du Vin de France,* has been very vocal about this issue, insisting that "about ninety percent" of all wine made in Burgundy is simultaneously chaptalized and acidified.

To be sure, French authorities rattle the bars of the wine cellar occasionally to give the impression that Burgundy's integrity is intact. They went through a series of these public relations exercises in the 1980s. In 1989, for example, Bouchard Père & Fils was convicted of blending non-Burgundy wines and for simultaneous chaptalization and acidification. The defense for Bouchard insisted—with great credibility—that their prosecution was unfair because they were singled out and made an example for doing what everyone else was doing. The French authorities who prosecuted them in court did not dispute this.

In Bordeaux, as this book was being completed, a French judicial inquiry investigated whether Château Giscours in the prestigious Margaux region illegally doctored the wines in its Grand-Giscours brand by adding water and organic acids, mixing vintages, and using forbidden filtering agents. A second investigation into a previous complaint that the winery used oak chips instead of barrels for aging the wine (illegal there, legal in the U.S.) is still continuing. Giscours has maintained that it has done nothing that is not common practice among other wineries.

Outright counterfeiting, meanwhile, given the high

prices and scarcity of Burgundy wine, for instance, is a lucrative business. French officials estimate that worldwide there is probably one counterfeit bottle of Domain Romanée-Conti for every genuine bottle. Most of those are sold in the United States or the Far East, primarily Japan and Hong Kong. French officials shrug off the fraud. "If they can't tell the difference, and they are not French, then it is not so much our problem," one high-ranking member of the OIV told me in 1997 over a glass of presumably genuine Gevrey-Chambertin at Vinexpo, the world's largest international wine trade show in Bordeaux.

French law enforcement officials also chose Vinexpo 1997 as the venue to announce one of the periodic convictions of Burgundy fraudsters. Turning the usual blind eye to the shenanigans at home, the French were proud that they had convinced a court in Bad Kreuznach, Germany, to convict a German grower and vintner of counterfeiting Chablis from non-Burgundian grapes and selling some 126,000 bottles of it through German retail stores in 1994.

The German counterfeiter, Jurgen Muller, will spend "at least several years in prison," according to the Bureau Interprofessionnel des Vins de Bourgogne (BIVB), which initiated the court case.

Many Americans will find the Chablis fight a confusing one and scratch their heads over why the French would get so worked up about defending cheap, sweet white wine. And that American confusion is the tip of wine fraud and deception in the United States.

The "Chablis" that most Americans know is among the lowest grades of cheap jug wines, made from whatever white wine happens to be left over. It is the sort of wine you serve to your guests when it is time for them to leave. Genuine French Chablis, on the other hand, is a remarkably delicious wine made from Chardonnay grapes grown in the Bourgogne near the town of Chablis.

In the early part of the twentieth century, Gallo and other large American producers appropriated a number of well-known European wine names such as Chablis, Burgundy, Beaujolais, Chianti, Champagne, and others for their own wines, which bore precious little resemblance to the European originals. This continues despite the fact that it is a crime in most of the rest of the world to produce and sell wines with those names without actually being a vintner in those regions and meeting the very strict rules governing their production. In many ways, this is tantamount to trademark theft, and the Europeans have fought it for decades. While the issue is over a geographic appellation name, an appellation is, in reality, a type of brand name that wineries and their associations try to build.

The common American opinion that Chablis is cheap sweet stuff is the best evidence that Gallo and the other wineries that misuse this regional brand name have destroyed the value of wine by that name. The French and other European Union nations have threatened boycotts of U.S. products, trade embargoes, and tariffs over this issue and continue to fight the misuse of their brands all over the world.

Gallo found itself on the losing side of the Chablis issue in 1997 when Japan barred the sale of Gallo "Chablis" following a survey of more than 20,000 wine retailers, restaurateurs, and sommeliers who said Gallo's practice was misleading. Gallo "Chablis" and "Hearty Burgundy" have been mainstays of the company's Japanese sales for more than two decades. The Japanese decision follows a similar 1995 Australian agreement with the European Union, which has banned the misappropriation of appellations for decades.

The Bureau of Alcohol, Tobacco and Firearms, which has jurisdiction over all wine labels, has done nothing to stop the misappropriation of appellation brands by Gallo and other wineries. The stand is hypocritical at best during a time when the U.S. government is pressuring China and other nations to cease their support for counterfeiters who rip off everything from the Windows 95 operating system to books, music, brand-name clothes, and even Mickey Mouse.

Playing fast and loose with names is a bait-and-switch tactic that is illegal in many areas of commerce. Though this is a common practice among American wineries, particularly the large ones, it is nevertheless misleading and deceptive.

The use of the name "Champagne" in the United States is a good example. In Europe or most of the rest of the world, it is illegal to call a sparkling wine "Champagne" unless it was made according to a rigorous set of standards in the Champagne region of France. Part of those standards involve what is called the *methode champenoise,* in which the wine undergoes two fermentations, one from grapes to still wine and then a secondary bottle fermentation which produces the bubbles. This is a labor-intensive, time-consuming process in which each of the bottles (capped with a beer-bottle-like cap instead of a cork) is stored in racks with the neck at a downward angle. Periodically, a worker known as a "riddler" gives each bottle an abrupt partial turn which causes the dead yeast cells (from the secondary fermentation) to migrate toward the mouth of the bottle. During this time, the sparkling wine also picks up the toasty, faint caramel chocolate taste of the yeast cells.

The process of riddling is repeated over and over for almost two years. Eventually the yeast forms a plug at the mouth of the bottle. The necks of the bottles are then frozen and a worker uncaps the bottle cap and allows the pressure inside the unfrozen rest of the bottle to shoot the yeast plug out. The bottle is then topped up with a small amount of the appropriate still wine and then corked and finished with the little wire basket and foil.

All of this improves the taste of the Champagne and increases the production costs and retail price on wines made this way, whether they come from Champagne, other parts of France, or Napa Valley. The correct term for wine made by this method outside the Champagne region of France is "sparkling wine." Significantly, sparkling wine made in other parts of France—even to the same standards and from the same grapes—cannot be called Champagne and is instead called *vin mousseaux* (frothy wine).

There is a second, cheaper method for making sparkling wine called the "bulk method," which produces wine which is inferior to that made by *methode champenoise* but is nevertheless a workmanlike product, especially in fruit punches and mimosas at Sunday brunch. In this process, the secondary fermentation takes place in massive tanks where the yeast cells are removed with industrial pumps and filters and the wine is then bottled, mostly untouched by expensive human hands.

As Gallo and the other large producers have tried to turn this sow's ear into a silk purse, their marketing people first came up with a French name, Charmat, after the Frenchman who invented the process. Even though Gallo and others could legally (in the U.S.) call their sparkling wine Champagne, the labels had to specify that the wine in the bottles was made by the "Charmat Bulk Process" method.

In 1989, the National Association of Beverage Importers, which was handling genuine Champagne, wrote a complaint letter to the BATF to protest the use of the word "Champagne" by Gallo on its Tott's brand labels with the required modifiers: "Charmat Bulk Process." This started a brouhaha with Gallo, Canandaigua, the Wine Group, and Bronco Wine—responsible for almost all the bulk-process sparkling wine in America—on one side, and the beverage importers on the other, joined by the Classic Methods/Classic Varietals Association (CM/CV), representing almost every American winery making sparkling wine by the traditional *methode champenoise* and using the traditional mix of grapes.

Gallo and its allies wanted to eliminate the use of "bulk process" because they thought it was demeaning. They argued that "Charmat" was descriptive enough, despite the fact that very few consumers have any idea what it means. The CM/CV people argued that bulk process sparkling wines are inherently inferior, having no toasty taste from the *sur lies* because they are aged for four months or less, and have a soda pop feel in the mouth from the very large carbonation-like bubbles rather than the foamy feeling from the smaller bubbles produced via *methode champenoise*.

In the end the big guys bullied their way to a winning position that confuses consumers and makes it harder for them to choose wisely. The 1988 Tott's bottle says on the label that it is "California Champagne" and that it is "Charmat Method Sparkling Wine: Secondary Fermentation Before Bottling."

The Tott's label is further misleading because it calls the wine in the bottle "Reserve Cuvée," which makes many people think it is something special when in reality "reserve" is an unregulated term and can be applied equally to plonk or prized wine. The final meaningless point of confusion is the phrase "Naturally Fermented" on the neck label. All sparkling wine is naturally fermented regardless of method. This marketing hype is the same sort of practice that got food companies in trouble with the federal government several years ago when they began putting "fat free" and similar words on foods that had never contained fat.

The practice is legal, but it is certainly anticonsumer and shows contempt for the customer. I have mentioned Tott's here only because it is the brand that started the controversy ten years ago, but it is not alone. An examination of other American bulk process sparkling wine labels will show the same misleading packaging.

Another controversy over potentially misleading labels and their associated advertisements erupted in October 1996 when BATF inspectors ordered a halt to the bottling of wine carrying the label of Rutherford Vineyards, owned by Central Valley wine giant Bronco Wine Company. The federal action was initiated by complaints by Napa Valley vintners who felt the Rutherford Vintner's label and its ad campaign were deceptive and intended to mislead consumers into thinking that the wine in the bottles came from the Rutherford appellation in Napa Valley, one of the most prestigious winegrowing areas in California.

Financial gain is mostly what American Viticultural

Areas (the U.S. term for an appellation) are all about to begin with. These appellations are supposed to define specific areas with unique soils, microclimates, and growing conditions that impart characteristic flavors and qualities to wine made from their grapes. By and large the appellations have been drawn in a manner that loosely follows this mandate. But beneath the glowing words about the "terroir" (French concept that grape taste comes from the soil) and the fawningly esoteric descriptions of the various appellations, under the genteel masquerade there is cold hard cash at stake. In California as in France, the highest-rated vineyards fetch the highest prices, and wine made from them fetch higher prices still.

The Napa Valley vintners have a valid point about Bronco's clever twisting of the appellation laws. The fact is, they also take advantage of the appellation rules for their own advantage; after all, they are the ones who fought so hard for the appellation to begin with, an appellation that they knew would help them market wines from their area and get higher prices for it.

But because so many small premium vintners have a hard time admitting that they must actually pay homage to commerce, they failed to make the strongest point about Bronco's use of the Rutherford name. By creating the impression that the inferior wine in the Rutherford Vineyard's bottles came from Rutherford, in Napa, Bronco's actions had the potential for degrading the value of this appellation and decreasing the premium for wines bearing the name. In fact, the Chardonnay carries the "California" appellation on the label, rather than "Napa" or "Sonoma," a tip-off that the wine most likely came from the Central Valley. But the rest of the packaging, the advertisement, and even the case boxes prominently emphasize "Rutherford, Napa Valley," which creates—even for the knowledgeable wine consumer—the impression that this is a Napa Valley wine when it is not.

The truth is, there is no winery for Rutherford Vineyards. There was once a winery named Rutherford Vintners, owned by Bernard Skoda. But in 1994, after Skoda died, Bronco (owned by the Franzia family of Ceres, in California's Central Valley) bought the brand—the rights to the label, not the winery—and changed the name to Rutherford Vineyards. The wine in the Rutherford Vineyards bottles was bulk wine, hauled in by tanker truck from wherever the grapes were crushed and fermented. Then, in a common practice, they contracted two area wineries with excess bottling line capacity to bottle the wine for Bronco.

This is essentially what a negociant does in France, a time-honored practice that can produce fine wine depending on how the purchased bulk wine is treated, blended, and cellared. Indeed, like most of Bronco's wines, the Rutherford Vineyards Chardonnay is a pretty good value, but only at $5 per bottle. What's more, the quality is equal to the worst wine made by the least talented of wineries in the Rutherford appellation, which also get a financial free ride from keeping the Rutherford appellation prestigious and the production limited. For, in addition to the marketing and promotional value of the name, the strict geographic boundaries of the appellation mean that only a finite amount of grapes can be produced within it. Limited supply helps create higher prices even for the weak-link wineries that are located within the boundaries.

The vintners' complaints noted that the 125,000 cases of Rutherford Vineyards Chardonnay is greater than the entire production of the entire Rutherford appellation. So, even though there are a few second-rate wineries within this appellation which make wine of equal or lesser quality to Bronco's Rutherford Vineyards, the true damage is done by flooding the market and making Rutherford appellation wine seem less restricted than it truly is.

In February 1997, just four months after the BATF halted production of Rutherford Vineyards Chardonnay, the district attorneys of Napa, Sonoma, and Mendocino counties began investigating the circumstances with an eye to filing suit over unfair business practices and misleading advertising. "Somebody who's a real snob about wine might look at every word on the bottle," said Sonoma County Deputy District Attorney Dave Copenhaver. "But the average person will see Napa Valley and expect Napa Valley wine."

As of early 1998, Bronco is still appealing the BATF's actions, but the issue with the district attorneys was resolved in April 1997 when Bronco agreed to post shelf signs stating that the grapes in Rutherford Vineyards came from the Central Valley.

Wine buyers need to be aware that outright grape fraud could play a role in that bottle of Cabernet that doesn't quite taste like a Cabernet. In fact, it may have been made with cheaper grapes. Indeed, Fred Franzia pleaded guilty to grape fraud in 1993, the largest fish caught by investigators who nabbed a dozen California growers for defrauding wineries by selling cheap or lower grade wine and grapes as more expensive varietals.

According to Assistant U.S. Attorney Steven Lapham of Sacramento, California, who prosecuted the case, Franzia admitted being involved in a scheme to sell cheap, generic red grapes as more costly Cabernet Sauvignon and Zinfandel varieties. Grape fraud has great financial potential. In 1992 the California Department of Agriculture's official grape crush report said that the average price for Fresno County (a major Central Valley wine grape region) red wine of all types was about $200 per ton, while Cabernet Sauvignon was going for $387 per ton and Zinfandel $332.

Federal prosecutor Lapham says the grape scam worked this way: Franzia purchased less expensive red grapes such as Carigane or Grenache (both about $196 per ton in 1992) from growers, and told either the growers or Bronco staff to create field documentation which misrepresented the grapes as more expensive Zinfandel or Cabernet Sauvignon. This fraudulent documentation would then be given to wineries purchasing the wine that Bronco would make from the grapes on their behalf.

Franzia further doctored the documentation to make it almost impossible to trace the grapes back to their true origin by making the payments for the purchased grapes to a nonexistent third party instead of the actual vineyards supplying the grapes. This made it appear that the grapes had been brokered by a third party.

A final consumer deception pitfall for consumers lies in many "box wines"—brick-like four-liter, plastic-lined cardboard containers which are sometimes filled with something akin to wine Kool Aid instead of pure wine.

Wines in a box have been around for more than thirty years, having been pioneered in Australia and long accepted there by consumers. In theory, it is a good way to store and serve wine because the plastic membrane inside the box collapses as wine is dispensed, thus preventing the introduction of air which can oxidize and spoil the wine.

While the wine box seems like the perfect container for inexpensive everyday wine, in reality most of the boxes you see are adulterated with substantial quantities of added alcohol, water, citric acid, fruit juices, and other flavors and chemicals. In practice, under a strict interpretation of BATF rules, a box of this sort could contain as little as 38 percent wine.

The issue came to a head in May 1997 when the BATF announced that it was scrutinizing labels used by Canandaigua on its Almaden brand "Winemaster White" boxed wines that had begun adding the California appellation and a varietal designation (the name of a grape—Chardonnay or Cabernet Sauvignon, for instance). Federal law requires that varietally labeled wines contain at least 75 percent of the designated wine grape by volume.

The California Association of Winegrape Growers urged the BATF to tighten up its label requirements and said: "We believe these kinds of its labels have a negative impact on the U.S. varietal integrity program."

As *beverages*, none of these formula products are wholly unpalatable, but most are clearly inferior to even the least expensive jug wines. And to be honest, these are not wines, but rather wine-cooler-type beverages. The manufacturers of these concoctions will argue that their labels describe the contents honestly. But in reality the language on the labels is as misleading as that tacked on to bulk process sparkling wine, and the images of refreshing glasses of *wine* on the box would lead most consumers to think the box contained . . . well, wine.

With the BATF most certainly tightening the requirements, you can be sure that any box with a fanciful name like "Winemaster White" and no appellation or varietal designation will contain less than 75 percent wine. On the other hand, even with varietal and appellation designations, there is ample room for adulteration with the chemical stew that makes for a "formula wine."

Because most box wines will contain substantial amounts of nonwine components, consumers are much better off avoiding them entirely. Instead, they will be better off buying jug wines or the least expensive wine in standard 750ml bottles.

PART II

Investing in Wine

As we have seen in previous chapters, the wine industry is a modest business segment run by a contentious confederation of dreamers, divas, and dictators who make a beverage that just happens to foster the most captivating and historically celebrated sensory experience of all time save that of sex.

Wine and sex are alike in many different ways: they can both be intoxicating, expensive, and cause a loss of control. Engaged in sensibly, both offer hours of enjoyment and are good for your health and emotional welfare. Abused, they can bring down governments and kingdoms and ruin personal finances and relationships.

Both wine and sex are best enjoyed for the sake of the love involved instead of the money. After almost thirty years of drinking wine and twenty years of working in the industry as a journalist, importer, and wholesaler, I can say that you had *better* love wine because there is relatively little money to be made, and it is made by a very small handful of people.

Unlike technology IPOs, which have made millionaires out of secretaries and production line workers, the few wineries that have gone public have not spun off legions of millionaires among the cellar rats and field workers. Instead, in every case, a handful of people at the top—family members (Mondavi, Canandaigua) or corporate/financial insiders (Beringer, Chalone)—have reaped the benefits.

Technology has spread wealth with an egalitarian hand, enriching the labor that made the companies successful. Immigrants have realized their American dreams in technology even while holding counterfeit green cards. This has not happened in the wine industry, but not because the insiders are more selfish than their technology counterparts. The truth is that there simply is not as much wine wealth to spread around. Plus, technology creates its own financial weather, growing the market by billions every day, while wine is lucky to hold its own market share against beer and spirits on a good day. When you're not creating new wealth every day, there simply isn't as much wealth to spread around to workers, investors, or stockholders.

It's simple: invest in technology for the money, not the love; in wine for the love, not the money.

This is not a warning against investing in either wine or the companies that produce it. The right investment can offer hours and years of enjoyment and reward. Just do it with your eyes (instead of your wallet) wide open and your investment goals focused on the horizon of pleasure rather than profit.

EIGHT

From the Dirt to the Bottle

FARMERS EVERYWHERE DO THEIR JOBS FOR THE LOVE AND NOT the money. Certainly there are are absentee corporate landowners who sit in their nice offices and fret about a spot of dirt on their Guccis and are more familiar with the controls of a Jaguar than a John Deere, but they are not farmers.

I mean real farmers with mud on their boots and a passion for the land in their hearts. People who are *that* smart, and willing to work *that* hard, and who have the courage and determination to outlast floods, droughts, pestilence, arbitrary markets, scheming customers, and all the rest of the worst that heaven and earth can throw their way, obviously have enough of the right stuff to make more money doing almost anything else. And yet, they love the land and they persist.

Growers, as vineyard owners are known in wine country, are no different. It's just that their crop is viewed by outsiders as a bit more glamorous than the prunes, walnuts, cattle, and other crops that grew on the land before the vineyards came. But the process of growing wine grapes is agriculture, and that takes dirt and dedication. Just as you are never farther away from agriculture than your next meal, your wine is only as good as the grapes that the vine produced from soil and water and air.

Wringing a living—much less a profit—from the ground is one of the toughest things in the world to do on a consistent basis, tougher than writing software, tougher than designing a new computer. Programmers who write mediocre software can make millions, but a mediocre farmer is usually one looking for a job in town. Only the very best vineyard owners and operators who work with the most desired grape varietals in the very best appellations with the very best weather, and who manage to avoid devastation from natural disasters or pests, can produce financial returns acceptable to institutional investors. Just a few of the luckiest of the elite growers and vineyard managers can produce an annual return (known as an Internal Rate of Return) of twelve percent or more. It is much harder for an investor to find a vineyard returning, say, fifteen percent, than it is to find an office building or light industrial park with this level of return. And far more can go wrong far faster with a vineyard to cut its returns in half (or push it into loss territory) than with similar commercial properties.

Today, with the prices of vineyard land in Napa and Sonoma counties soaring, growers need to have good CPAs on their teams alongside the viticulturists, pest managers, and farm advisers. To see why, let's look at the basic economics of a vineyard.

An average Napa Valley vineyard costs about $34,000 per acre for the raw land and another $18,000 per acre to capitalize it (prepare the land, install trellising, irrigation, and plant rootstock). These and other figures came from interviews with growers, from California State Agriculture Department records, and with the help of Mike Fisher, CPA and partner in Motto, Kryla & Fisher in Napa Valley, the U.S. wine industry's preeminent accounting and financial consulting firm.

This vineyard financial model is my own approach aimed at simplifying things without sacrificing too much in accuracy. Keep in mind that financial projections are best guesses subject to weather and the other unexpected events that can render the finest models invalid.

That said, let's examine the assumptions underlying the model. The harvest tonnage will be slightly optimistic at 4.5 tons per acre. In reality, the ten-year (1986-96) average harvest for Napa County is 3.4 tons per acre for Cabernet Sauvignon, 4.2 for Merlot, and 4.0 for Chardonnay. I use a slightly higher figure here because many vineyards that fell to the Phylloxera debacle of the 1980s and 1990s are being replanted with more vines per acre—so the next thirty years (the life of the vineyard in this model) should mean a gradual increase in the tonnage per acre.

For premium vineyards, harvest tonnage is frequently limited by the grower's contracts with wineries. The upper limit a grower can produce is usually six tons per acre, because a larger production can result in dilution of flavors and overall decrease in wine quality. Overfertilizing and overwatering can boost quantity at the expense of quality, so many contracts specify a price penalty for the grower who overproduces—as much as ten percent for a five-to-ten-percent overproduction. A winery can even refuse to buy any grapes at all if the overproduction reaches twenty to thirty percent.

Long-term grape contracts can be a double-edged financial sword, and they reveal, in microcosm, the tension between growers (who want the highest prices and highest yields) and wineries (which try to pay the lowest prices possible). While contracts guarantee the winery access to the grapes and the grower a dependable income, it means that wineries can pay more for wines when there is an abundance, as there was in California in 1997, and growers can get too little if they are locked into prices when there is a shortage, such as in 1995-96.

Understanding vineyard economics can help you assess investment potential for winery and vineyard stocks. We'll see that a vineyard has many unvarying fixed costs; there are very few ways to economize when grape prices drop in years of abundance. So companies with many vineyards can be expected to perform better when grape supplies are tight and fare worse in times of abundance.

Contracts also specify such aspects as the sugar content at which the grapes are to be harvested (generally 22.5 to 24 Brix) and the right to refuse the grapes totally if the sugar drops below a certain level, generally 21 or 22 Brix. The winery can also dictate policy in such areas as pruning, fruit thinning, leaf pulling, irrigation, fertilization, pest control, and other vineyard practices. A grower's attempt to control costs can be neutralized by the winery's conditions for managing the vineyard.

In our model, the price paid for a ton of grapes is $1,717, the overall average for all Napa County grapes of all varietals paid in 1997, according to the California State Crush Report. These are the most expensive grapes in the state. This price is probably high, since many wineries signed contracts with growers at record prices due to the grape shortages of 1995-96, not knowing that 1997 would see a record harvest.

Still, vineyard owners with prized land in such prestigious appellations as Rutherford and Stag's Leap in Napa County and Dry Creek Valley and Sonoma Mountain in Sonoma County can often command 50 to 100 percent more per ton for their grapes.

In addition, a grower will usually get more for grapes that are made into "single vineyard designate" wine. You'll see this on labels such as "Kenwood, Jack London Vineyards," where the name of a vineyard appears on the label. These single grapes are judged by the winemaker to have a unique character and ability to make superior wines . . . at superior prices, of course.

A change in grape prices of as little as $50 per ton can affect the overall return of the vineyard by a full percentage point. Likewise, relatively small changes in the more prosaic areas of overhead (paperwork, overall management) and agricultural maintenance (pruning, pest control, trellis and irrigation maintenance, etc.) can move yields up or down by one or two points.

A vineyard fetching $1,800 per ton for grapes can easily lose money if overhead and maintenance are at the high end of the range, a difference of about $1,000 per year per acre.

Even more significant is the cost of harvesting, generally about $125 per ton. Increases here as small as $25 per ton can blow the bottom out of the overall yield. California growers have had a relatively gentle relation-

ship with farm workers—mostly Hispanic immigrants
or undocumented workers—which is by no means
guaranteed for the future. Unionization efforts could
drive harvest and maintenance costs up substantially.
And even though Napa and Sonoma growers rely increasingly on year-round workers as opposed to mi-
grants, crackdowns in 1996 and 1997 by the U.S.
Immigration and Naturalization Service could shrink
the labor pool, thus pushing wages higher even in the
absence of union efforts. When there is such a wide
variation in profits from relatively small amounts of
money, it is clear that there is not much margin for
error.

Thus, it's little wonder that back in 1990 when the
industry was experiencing steady decreases in consumption, interest rates were soaring, and lenders were
getting hammered from the real estate crash, banks re-
acted by cutting off credit to vineyards and wineries.
At that time, about one-third of all California vineyards
were losing money. By 1997, thanks to record prices
and harvests, almost all vineyards made money. But
profitability also depends on many different factors
over which a grower has no influence whatsoever, including interest rates.

The cost of money is crucial. Because of the very
low and stable interest rates of the mid- and late nine-
ties, people have been lulled into complacency about
the dangers of debt. This has resulted in many vineyard
and winery operations borrowing more money than
would be prudent were interest rates higher. At this
point, even small increases in interest costs can bank-
rupt a vineyard. Federal Reserve Board Chairman
Alan Greenspan has stated that interest rate increases
are eventually inevitable. And when rates go up, the

first to go under will be vineyards that have high debt loads.

In the financing of the land and capitalization, my model differs somewhat from actual practice for the sake of simplicity. In 1998 a farmer developing a new vineyard could borrow up to 70 percent of the appraised value of the land and improvements at a rate of 8 to 10 percent annual interest. For simplicity, let us assume that this could be borrowed for the thirty-year life of the vineyard with no payback of principal. In reality, things are a bit tougher: a commercial bank will typically loan for a period of twenty years and will require payment of interest and principal, but a financially adept vineyard owner can shop for rates and terms and refinance when necessary to produce the best results, which won't differ too much from our simpler model. No one knows how long interest rates will remain as low as they were in 1998. But a one percent increase in rates from 8 percent in my model to 9 percent can cut the yield by a third. A three percent increase shoves a vineyard into the loss category, even with all other factors remaining the same.

We also assume that the grower can obtain financing to sustain the vineyard operations through the incomeless first three years after planting, when no commercial crop is produced by the new vines, and spread this loss over the life of the vineyard. Finally, we assume that the grower sells the vineyard at the end of thirty years with an appreciation of the land (on the equity 30 percent) added into the overall return.

Since interest in my model is the single largest annual expense, growers who already own their land and convert to grapes from other agricultural uses will have the largest profits, or the greatest room for error. This also means that anyone trying to buy into the vineyard business faces an uphill financial battle.

Wineries like to give vineyard ownership a positive spin, insisting that it allows control of wine grape availability, quality, and costs, most important in higher end wines where the competition for particular vineyards can be intense. In times of grape scarcity and rising prices, a winery can benefit from control of its own vineyards, but this still may not justify the capital expenditure. Beringer's initial public offering prospectus, for example, said that in 1996 (a year of tight grape supplies and shortages), the average cost per ton of producing Chardonnay grapes on the company's Santa Barbara vineyards was $825, compared to a weighted average price paid for Santa Barbara Chardonnay grapes of $1,450.

Assuming a yield of 4.5 tons, the company saved $2,815 per acre by growing its own grapes vs. buying them on contract. By comparison, that acre of developed vineyard, while less expensive than Napa or Sonoma, would cost about $30,000. So it would take Beringer nearly eleven years to break even by growing its own grapes instead of buying them.

Further, most harvest years have not seen grape shortages, so the winery might never recover its costs during the life of the vineyard, especially if it needed early replanting due to Phylloxera or some other pest. To the company and stockholders, their capital would fetch a lower return than it would at a company not burdened with as many vineyards. This is further complicated by the current period of oversupply the industry is entering, where falling prices and a glut of wine favor wineries with few of their own vineyards.

The owners of vineyards—whether they be wineries

or growers—must accept a rate of return that counts as average to mediocre, and a risk that rates as extremely high when compared with other real estate investments. There's only one reason for such relatively imprudent investing: for the love.

NINE

From the Grape to Your Lips

DEFINING A WINERY IS A LOT LIKE DEFINING A DOG. A DOG can be a dachshund or Dalmatian, a rottweiler or golden retriever. Wineries are similarly diverse. A winery can own vineyards or own none and buy its grapes from a grower. It can own everything it takes to make wine, from the crusher/destemmer to the fermenting tanks, aging tanks, barrels, and bottling line. Or it can rent some or most of these, even be a winery without owning anything at all, a process known as custom crushing or custom winemaking.

Winemaking is part art and part science. Given the same grapes from the same vineyard and the same facilities, no two winemakers will make the same wine. And given the finest grapes from the finest appellation, the winemaker is the difference between a very good wine and a world-class wine, one that sells for $15 and another that can bring $50 or more.

Winemakers will make a thousand decisions involving tanks, barrels, fermentation, aging times, and more, all of which determine the cost of producing the wine and its ultimate price to the consumer. After fermentation and aging, the wine is either bottled, corked, labeled and boxed, thus producing "case goods," or sold on the bulk marketplace.

The cost of grapes is the most expensive single item in most bottles of wine. A ton of grapes crushed for premium wine produces about 142 gallons, and there are 2.36 gallons in each twelve-bottle case. (Each bottle is 750 milliliters; an easy rule of thumb is that five bottles are almost exactly equal to one gallon.) A single vine typically produces just about a gallon of wine, although viticulturists usually measure vine output in pounds (usually 13 to 15 pounds of grapes per vine). While vineyard spacing and trellising can vary the yield, it takes roughly 142 vines to produce a ton of grapes.

That ton produces 60 twelve-bottle cases, for a total of 720 bottles. So you can calculate the cost of grapes in a bottle of wine by dividing the per-ton price by 720. From grapes costing $1,300 per ton, for example, each bottle would contain about $1.80 worth of grape juice. Yet wine made from those grapes is unlikely to retail for less than $15 or $18. So where does the money go?

First of all, there is tremendous potential variation in cost. The grapes could cost $274 per ton if they come from Fresno and $4,000 per ton from some very elite Napa or Sonoma vineyards. The actual glass bottle can cost 20 to 50 cents or even more, depending on the weight and style. A humble cork can cost from 8 cents to 25 cents, labels from 2 cents to 25 cents. If the bottle has a foil (the thing you cut off to get to the cork) it can cost up to 13 cents.

This means the range of raw material costs per bottle looks like this:

	MOST EXPENSIVE	LEAST EXPENSIVE
Grapes	$6.00	$0.50
Bottle	0.50	0.20
Cork	0.25	0.08
Foil	0.13	0.00
Label	0.25	0.02
Bottling, corking	0.25	0.17
Total	$7.37	$0.97

Yet the most expensive bottles of California wine typically retail for $50 to $100 per bottle, and the least expensive cork-finished wines rarely cost less than $4 per bottle. Clearly there is a lot more that goes into the price of your wine. So where does it really go? You may be surprised.

Let's look at two real-life bottles of Chardonnay, one that retails for $18, and a more affordable one lower down on the shelf at $8. Most of the numbers presented below were developed by the accounting firm of Motto, Kryla & Fisher (MKF), and I am grateful for their permission to use their numbers.

A TALE OF TWO CHARDONNAYS:
PART I, PRODUCT COST

	$18 PER BOTTLE	$8 PER BOTTLE
Bottling	$0.75	$0.50
Oak Aging	0.42	0.08

	$18 PER BOTTLE	$8 PER BOTTLE
Aging	0.67	0.17
Winemaking	0.75	0.33
Grapes	1.74	1.00
Total	$4.33	$2.08
	($52/case)	($25/case)

This reflects a middle of the road choice on bottles, corks, foils, and labels for the $18 wine and a fairly rock bottom choice for the $8 bottle. The grapes in the $18 bottle would cost about $1,300 per ton, while a ton of those in the $8 bottle of wine would cost $742.

Next on the list of product costs is oak aging. Oak helps alter the chemical balance of wine, imparting flavors that are often interpreted as "toasty" or vanilla-like. Traditionally, oak aging meant using French oak barrels, which typically cost about $600 and hold approximately 25 cases of wine. This huge cost has prompted two new industries: (1) barrels made from American oak ($300 each), and (2) alternate ways of imparting the oak taste, including oak slats, pellets, or even chips bound up in very large tea bags.

Significantly, oak barrels "use up" their effectiveness with each vintage and impart slightly different flavors as they themselves age. This complicates the winemaker's task. Some wines may see a month in new oak barrels, and then a longer period of time in two- or three-year-old barrels, depending on what effects the winemaker is shooting for. The $18 Chardonnay in our example above mostly likely saw some aging time in a barrel, while the $8 bottle got a tea bag sloshed around in it for a while.

The aging and winemaking costs in our examples are both mainly functions of time, labor, and capital equipment. Our Chardonnay needs to age somewhere, either in tanks or barrels. The storage facilities cost money, and money costs money (interest). In addition, the aging process usually involves the labor costs of stirring the wine, moving it from one tank or barrel to another (called "racking"), and removing cloudiness through filtering and fining. Red wine is even more expensive, since it ages for two or three years longer than comparable white wine.

The winemaking portion of our example includes the crushing and fermentation of the wine, stirring of the must (accomplished by pumping wine over the hard "cap" of skins and seeds or by manually punching the cap into the juice with a stick). Next comes the removal of skins and seeds, pressing, and other labor- and capital-intensive tasks.

The $18 Chardonnay obviously sees a lot more attention in the aging and winemaking cycle than does the $8 bottle. But when we come to the total product cost, we find a winery still has only $4.33 in the $18 bottle and $2.08 in the $8 bottle. Where does the rest of the money go?

A TALE OF TWO CHARDONNAYS:
PART II, WINERY COST & PROFIT

	$18 PER BOTTLE	$8 PER BOTTLE
Profit	$0.83	$0.33
Income taxes	0.58	0.25
Interest	0.83	0.25
Administration	0.83	0.25
Marketing/Sales	2.08	0.92
Product (wine)	4.33	2.08
Total	$9.48	$4.08
	($114/case)	($49/case)

As you can see, the price of the wine when it leaves the winery is just a bit over half of what you pay for it. The rest of the price comes from distributor/wholesaler and retailer markups.

A TALE OF TWO CHARDONNAYS:
PART III, MARKUPS

	$18 PER BOTTLE	$8 PER BOTTLE
Winery	$ 9.48	$4.08
Wholesaler	2.90	1.33
Retailer	5.62	2.59
Total	$18.00	$8.00

When markups are considered in this equation, it is not hard to realize why wineries, especially smaller ones, are fighting so hard for the right to ship directly to you. A winery can double its profit by selling to you directly rather than through the traditional three-tier system.

Beware, however, of thinking that you're getting a better deal when you buy wine at most winery tasting rooms. With the exception of a very few enlightened tasting rooms, you will usually pay at or near suggested retail prices. Locals, who tend to be pretty thrifty folk in the wine country, know that you can almost always find the very same wine for substantially less at the local supermarket—even considering the tasting room's case discount.

Even clearer than the relatively large percentage that goes into markups is the enormous profit in those $50- or $125-per-bottles from small trendy wineries.

If we take the upper-end costs of $6.86 per bottle that we figured above using $4,000 grapes and an ex-

TEN

Your Own Portfolio of Liquid Assets

IT'S HARD TO ESCAPE NEWS REPORTS LIKE THE ONE ABOUT the case of 1945 Mouton that originally sold for about $20 and went at auction for $63,000, or how $500 cases of 1982 classified first growths of Bordeaux are now selling for $2,000 to $6,000, sometimes higher. It's easy to imagine the labels of your favorite fine wine as tasty stock certificates, convertible into either fat profits or pure pleasure.

But while there are certainly profits to be made on a relatively small number of wines, no honest person in the wine or investment business would advise that you stake your IRA or your kid's education on something that comes in a bottle. Wines are harder to sell than securities, require a precise storage environment, can go bad, need near-anal-retentive record keeping to

fetch top dollar, and involve hidden expenses and hassles unassociated with most other investments.

What's more, the Asian economic slump that hammered stocks in 1998 showed that prices do not always
move smoothly or reliably upward. The global financial
meltdown of 1998 sent a lot of people looking for a stiff
drink, but it's been a truly sobering experience for wine
connoisseurs who invested in the liquid assets of their
favorite French châteaux in the previous year or two.
Auction sale prices for some of the most expensive
wines fell by as much as 40 percent.

A historical analysis of recent auction prices at the
Chicago Wine Company (the only auction company
that makes all of its "hammer prices" available online
at www.tcwc.com/pauct.htm) reveals some pretty dramatic price variations, with older vintage prices dropping or remaining the same and younger ones showing
some respectable appreciations.

The bad news: Château Petrus 1982 sold for $1,533
per bottle in August 1997 and for $900 in August 1998,
a 42 percent plunge. Many winery stocks did as bad or
worse: Beringer dropped 42 percent from April to August 1998, and Mondavi has left a big crater, down 63
percent from October 1997 to August 1998. Other 1982
vintage comparisons (like other winery stocks) are bad
but not as extreme. The comparisons (1997/1998) include: Margaux $466/$410; Latour $483/$483; Lafite-
Rothschild $433/$370; Cheval Blanc $533/$480; Haut-
Brion $258/$266.

Now the good news: 1995 Lafite-Rothschild sold for
$150 in August 1997 and $250 a year later. Many other
1995 classified first growths showed similar appreciation, with only a few (Haut-Brion) showing no changes
(but no declines).

The effect on wine prices from the Asian economic meltdown took many by surprise, including venerable Christie's. In December 1997, when the famed London auction house put a lot of 1982 Mouton-Rothschild on the block, it failed to find any bidders at all at the offering price of about $7,380. As reported by trade newsletter *Global Wine News*, that auction saw eleven bottles of 1989 Château Le Pin go for $581 per bottle; a year before, the same wine fetched $1,230.

"Expectations were a bit high then," acknowledges Christopher Burr, international head of Christie's wine department. "But I think we and the rest of the market have adapted." Burr said he feels that these price dips are only temporary, and therefore represent a good opportunity. "If I were a young buyer, I'd be adding wines from the 1982, '86, and '90 vintages right now." Peter Duffey, manager of the Chicago Wine Company, agrees, but advises collectors to go after younger vintages. "I think 1995 and '96 are winners; you can almost guarantee the prices are going up." Burr, on the other hand, doesn't encourage people to speculate in wine. "It's a perishable product which should be enjoyed with friends," he said. "I do know a number of people who have profited by selling their excess inventory, but overall there are many better investment opportunities than wine."

These price drops, however, represent an opportunity over the next two to five years, since most economic analysts anticipate it will take at least that long for Asian economies to recover. And why is Asia important in this equation? Because the economies of Japan and other Asian nations soared in the 1980s and early 1990s. With wallets limber, Asian investors, led by the Japanese, went on a global buying spree that snapped up so much American real estate—especially on the West Coast—and so many companies that politicians were actively debating some sort of controls or barriers.

What does this have to do with wine? Everything. Flush with acquisitions, status-conscious Asian buyers then went after the lifestyle that befitted the new tycoons. They immediately zeroed in on French First Growth wines and helped bid up prices to new records. These soaring prices were boosted further by the strong economy in the United States, where successful investors also went after the big name French châteaux.

Investment-grade wines of all sorts were snapped up at record prices. Cellars were filled. Then, in late 1997, the Asian economies hit the wall; the hammering continued in 1998. Asian wine buyers became scarcer. Asian-owned real estate began hitting the market on the U.S. West Coast in August 1998 as investors looked for badly needed cash. It's no accident that many of the same people are now trying to unload their wine cellars.

This downturn in the Asian economy illustrates that the very three factors that make certain wines expensive—quality, scarcity, and hype—make their prices fragile. Surprisingly, quality is the least of these characteristics. As Frank Prial, the intelligent, down-to-earth wine columnist for the *New York Times*, writes, "Quality drives price, but not as much as scarcity. In the monied world where these wines are sold, the scarcer the wine, the more people want to buy it."

Another very smart wine writer, Dan Berger, points out that even without the Asian economic crisis, demand for investment-grade wines would be leveling off today naturally, since most people who could afford the wine have stocked their cellars to the rafters.

The production of many wines selling for $100 or $700 per bottle is typically less than 5,000 cases, sometimes as low as 2,500 cases. Are these the maximum amounts that these wineries can produce? Of course not. But like the diamond trade, where artificial scarcity keeps prices high, increasing production would only lower prices and profit margins. Remember your winery math: the higher the price, the greater the margin. Grapes, bottles, and corks cost only so much; this means that above the $30 level, each additional dollar of price is overwhelmingly profit.

Obviously quality counts, but as Prial, Berger, and others point out, a wine that costs $100 per bottle is not necessarily ten times better than a wine that costs $10. There are abundant wines on the market that are as good or better than the expensive names, will age as well or longer, and cost a fraction of the price of the overhyped, over-lusted-for big names. But Prial and very few others notwithstanding, wine writers in general are *not* your best friends when it comes to selecting the best wines for the price. They are all too frequently boosters of the system and true believers in the myths that perpetuate obscenely priced wines whose prices bear only a passing resemblance to their quality.

The iconization of old or trendy wineries that sell scarce wine for outrageous prices is common among most U.S. consumer wine magazines. (*Decanter*, a British publication, is far less afflicted with this sort of tripe.) Blinded by what they see as a divine light coming from the bottle, most American wine magazines play the willing dupe in the third factor that keeps prices on some wines far higher than their quality would merit: hype.

Longtime New York wine merchant Bill Sokolin puts hype near the top of his list for defining what makes for what he calls "investment grade wine." In his invaluable 1986 book, *Liquid Assets*, Sokolin says that "history, myth and passion always provoke our interest . . . wines with a reputation will eventually cost more." He recommends that before investing in a wine, one should first make sure the owner has a captivating manner and is willing to spend endless hours promoting and hyping his wine. "Investment value will often depend on whether the owner is willing to cultivate publicity and distribution."

Quality, scarcity, and hype. These are the rules that govern investing in rare wine, and it doesn't matter whether you think the rules make sense or not, you need to play by them if you're going to profit. After all, if you (and others) are buying wines whose prices are artificially inflated by hype and scarcity, you are going to have to sell those wines to another person who has bought into the same myth. You need to make sure the myth is perpetuated so you don't lose your investment.

One of the biggest myths is that old wine is better. No-nonsense wine columnist Frank Prial put it best when he told *Forbes* magazine: "Several years ago, I went to the Lafite-Rothschild Château, and over the course of a weekend, I tasted everything they had made since the family bought the place in 1868. With some of the older vintages still in the château cellars, they had to open three bottles to get one that was drinkable. If I were a collector, I would not open anything older than 1945, because it probably wouldn't be any good.

Besides, if I drank it, I'd lose the chance to unload it on someone else at auction."

Indeed, the best use for very old wine is to donate it to a charity auction and take the tax deduction, which is precisely the fate of the bottle of 1916 Château Margaux in my cellar which I bought at a charity auction to benefit an acquaintance who needed a liver transplant. In blunter terms, Doug Frost, MS/MW, derides the mythology of very old wines as "necrophilia."

But these myths must be perpetuated not only because there are millions of dollars at stake, but also because many of the people involved have built a large part of their personalities around the status symbol of owning expensive wine and of being part of the world elite that can afford and enjoy these scarce wines. "Mystique sells wine," Sokolin writes.

Indeed, top people in the investment quality field— people like Sokolin and Sherry-Lehmann chairman Michael Aaron—repeatedly advise clients to look at fine wine investment as a way to assure a dependable supply in future years of wines that they love, since they may then be outrageously priced, if available at all. In addition, if you buy more wine than you intend to drink, you'll have some bottles left over that can be bartered or sold for other wines.

So how do you set off on the adventurous trek to invest in wine? You'll need to figure out what to buy, where to buy it, how to store it, when to drink it, and who to sell it to (or through) when you decide to liquidate the asset in some way other than pouring it into a glass.

The first and best rule is to buy only those wines you love so much that you'd have no regrets if you were forced to drink them all yourself. But where, among the tens of thousands of wines in the world, do you start looking? If investment value is highly important to you, then the number of wines that have reliably stood the test of time is fairly small.

The vast majority of old, rare, fine and investment quality wines sold at auction are from the châteaux that came out as Premiers Grand Cru (First Great Growths) in the Paris Universal Exhibition classification of Bordeaux wines in 1855. While the classification has been termed an ossification by many (with some justification), there is also no doubt that these wines have stood the test of time. After all, Samuel Pepys was an Haut-Brion sipper back in 1663 when he penned some of his best work. Sixty years later, the highest-priced wines in London were still Haut-Brion, Lafite, Latour, and Margaux. These châteaux came out on top in the 1855 classification and they continue to rank among the very best today in terms of both quality and auction prices.

Toward the top of this category are Lafite-Rothschild, Latour, Margaux, Mouton-Rothschild, Haut-Brion, Ausone, Cheval Blanc, Petrus, Canon, Figeac, Magdelaine, Palmer, Ducru-Beaucallou, Leoville-Las-Cases, Pichon-Lalande, LaLagune, Certan de May, La Fleur Petrus.

The exceptions to the red Bordeaux domination?

- Sauternes (Châteaux d'Yquem, Climens, Rieussec)
- True vintage Ports (Taylor, Fonseca, Croft, Quinta do Noval, Graham, Warre, Dow, Sandeman, Cockburn)
- A few Burgundies (Romanée-Conti, La Tache, Richebourg)
- An occasional Rhone such as Guigal Côte Rotie

and a smattering of wines from:

- California (Mondavi, Opus One, Harlan Estate, Chateau Montelena, Clos du Val, Dunn)
- Italy (Sassacaia, Gaja Barbaresco, Biondi-Santi Brunello di Montalcino)
- Germany (Dr. Thanisch Bernlasteler Doktor, J.J. Prum Wehlener Sonnenuhr)

Of course, you can find wines for a fraction of these costs that will taste as good and age as long, but remember that if you're buying wine with an idea of eventually reselling it, you want those that have a ready market.

In California, there are a number of wines that have made a reputation as challengers for top auction spots. They still do not have a three-hundred-year-plus track record of longevity that is part of the mystique and hype that buoys the first growth market. This, of course, can be a good thing for you as you stock your cellar, since many California wines are every bit as good for the drinking but cost just a fraction. As competitions and taste-offs continue to show, the difference between the best California wines and the best French wines is more a matter of style and individual taste preference than quality. What's more, some California wines can show price appreciations of roughly the same magnitude as French, but cost much less per case than their French counterparts.

But beware: a number of wineries touted as the very top in the mid-1980s have fallen off the fast track, primarily from the inability to maintain quality. Among these California has-beens are: Heitz, Beaulieu (Georges de Latour), Jordan, Château St. Jean, Vichon, Sequoia Grove, and Chalone.

So, if you're aiming to satisfy both your palate and pocketbook, you need to select wines that you like to drink and which also fit into the select group that are lusted after by the Gucci herds. But how to experiment without losing your shirt, since these wines, because of their good investment potential, are necessarily expensive?

Some people try to mitigate the expense by splitting a bottle with a group at a fine restaurant. Sharing is the right idea, but the vast majority of restaurant wine is profoundly overpriced—three and often four times what it would cost at a retail store.

On the other hand, getting together with friends to share the expense (and experience) of really fine wine is a wonderful idea. You chip in and buy a $200-plus wine to sample and still have enough left over for hors d'oeuvres and a couple of very tasty $20 bottles to drink. Four is a good number for your group; six will stretch the bottle too thin to give the tasters more than a perfunctory sip or two. Remember, this should be fun. The entertainment you get from this is a real bargain compared to tickets to the theater or a professional sports event.

Do this twice a month and you can work your way through most of the top investment quality wines in less than a year. Don't complicate things by feeling you have to set an altar for this goddess of wine. Just drink the stuff like you would any other wine. If you fall in love, it could be an investment. If you have to convince yourself that you like it, then move on. Let your heart and your personal palate be your guides.

Your group can keep an eye on the auction market

to see what wines are hot. Better still, rely on someone who does that for a living: a good, trusted wine merchant. You can also spend some time on the Internet surfing some very good Web pages, many of which are posted by individuals out of their love of the subject. There is also a very good news group, alt.food.wine, which has a lively discussion of all sorts and where you can post your questions. America Online and CompuServe have very good wine forums and discussion groups, including occasional real-time chats.

If you want to see maximum appreciation of the value of your investment, your best bet is to buy as early as you can. This means buying the wine directly from the winery when it is first released, or even better, buying wine futures. These are also known by some as the "opening prices." Unlike cattle or soybean futures, where you place your bets with a broker, there is no actual exchange on which wine futures are traded. Instead, it is a fairly informal cottage industry where a winery or retailer sells you the right to buy a quantity of wine when it is released, typically three to four years after the vintage date. It is not unusual for the futures of Classified First Growths to double or triple in the first two years after the opening price and then double again when the wine is finally released. For example, a futures contract for a case of 1995 Château Margaux sold for $1,099 in June 1996 at Zachy's Wine and Liquors in New York City. A year later the futures contract sold for $3,600.

Recognize that you *do* have to take possession of your wine, unlike people who trade in pork bellies who never expect to have a semi show up one day filled with a few tons of frozen bacon.

While buying futures can be the fastest road to wine

price appreciation, it is especially risky in two key areas: quality and security. Since futures on Bordeaux wines are typically offered for sale starting in April of the year following the harvest, no one has actually tasted the wine and no one actually knows for sure how good the wine will be when you get it home and open a bottle. The situation is further complicated by the French tendency to proclaim every harvest as "the vintage of the century." You will need to do a fair amount of reading to get a feeling for whether the weather and other conditions conspire to produce a potentially good vintage or a disastrous one. The best sources for this information will come from three publications: *Decanter*, best for assessing European vintages; *Wine Spectator*, best for assessing American vintages; and *Wine Market Report*, which reports the most current news as it happens from the U.S. and Europe.

Vintage quality aside, the cottage nature of wine futures holds a great deal of risk that you may not get your wine even after paying for the futures. In the securities business, commodities traders are subject to strict regulation by government agencies, have minimum capitalization requirements, and are required to carry insurance that would cover at least part of a customer's losses if the firm goes out of business. Not so wine futures. Your ability to get your wine is dependent entirely on the wine merchant's staying in business, and on the merchant's ability to get the wine through a leaky conduit that includes a host of middlemen (and women) who are mostly honest but who can be unpredictably bent—including ground shippers on both ends, distributors, customs brokers and agents, and freighters that sometimes sink or mysteriously disappear.

A wine merchant with a shaky profit picture or moth-eaten morals may simply go out of business. A reputable merchant may be victimized by conduit leaks summarized above. Both problems have occurred with more frequency than anyone in the industry cares to talk about.

You can minimize your risk by negotiating a partial payment for the futures, with the balance to be paid on delivery (Bill Sokolin recommends 20 to 30 percent down if your purchase is over $5,000). Another way is to deal with large, well-known fine wine merchants who have been dealing in futures for decades. If a freighter flying the South Molluccan flag disappears in the middle of the ocean (as one did in the mid-1980s with a shipment of Sokolin's wine), those merchants can absorb the blow, and those who have been selling futures for years frequently have the contacts to obtain alternate shipments.

Sokolin points out that if a shipment containing wine to satisfy futures contracts disappears, the most reputable merchants will first try to obtain the wine at any price to satisfy the customer. If the wine cannot be obtained, then a refund should be made *not* merely of the customer's money, but in the appreciated amount that the customer would have realized if the wine were sold upon delivery.

Obviously, the number of merchants that fit these criteria are a subset of those selling futures. While there are no guarantees, the safest sources from which Americans can buy European futures are probably all in New York City: Sokolin, Zachy's, Morrell, and Sherry-Lehmann.

Most American wineries don't have futures programs. The Robert Mondavi Winery was the first to offer futures and has the best developed program. In the U.S., futures are sold mostly by the wineries themselves without any intermediaries. Since these programs are not well marketed (like most everything else the American wine industry does), the best thing to do is ask your favorite winery if it sells futures.

If you find yourself on the losing end of a futures contract delivery, your options are limited to civil litigation or trying to get the local district attorney involved if you suspect illegality, as opposed to mere incompetence. You may not have even this to fall back on if you buy from a merchant who ships directly to you in contravention of direct shipping laws. You'll need to assess the risk of buying futures through a merchant in your own state (who can ship to you legally) who may not be as large and well-known as the New York firms, but against whom you'd have legal recourse if the deal crashed and burned. In any event, make sure you save all documentation, receipts, contracts, and any other data that can prove your right to collect the wine at the price you paid.

As you can see from the way futures can appreciate, the risks can be worth the rewards. On the other hand, futures may not be as lucrative over the next three to five years because of the instability in wine sales prices in general. Since futures are a present-day bet on the coming value of wine, it remains to be seen if futures prices will immediately drop to the same extent as wines that have already been released. Buying futures over the next three to five years will be an even greater gamble than in the past, because buyers will be betting on a significant upturn in the global economy at a time when most economists say a recession is more likely.

If you choose not to walk this route and want to

lay hands on the bottles immediately, you have the benefit of tasting notes that rate the wine, you have the ability to taste it yourself to decide if you like it. On the other hand, the price appreciations of already released wine could be minimal. Remember the 1995 Château Margaux above? It did most of its appreciating as a futures wine. Despite its perfect 100 rating by *Wine Spectator*, the price did not go up very much once the actual wine was delivered to stores: it was advertised for sale in early 1998 for $310 per bottle (or $3,720 per case). In addition, there are substantial expenses in selling your wine, as you'll see below.

You should again buy from a reputable source, preferably directly from the winery or someone who obtained it that way. This makes it easier to document the wine's "provenance"—vital for selling at top dollar since the buyer is assured that the wine has been cellared in a manner that will assure its longest possible life.

Another of the import industry's dirty secrets is that most wine is transported on ships in noninsulated and unrefrigerated containers, where it often bakes in broiling sun or shivers in freezing temperatures on the dock and on the deck for weeks. This includes a substantial amount of investment quality wines, most of which are transported from the winery to the docks in ordinary semi-trailers. If you want to show a potential buyer that your wine has been pampered, you'll need a statement from your wine merchant that the wine was shipped in a "reefer," along with a copy of the shipping documents to confirm that.

Once you have the wine, the pampering and provenance paper trail must continue until the day you sell it. Don't buy investment quality wine unless you have a proper place to store it. That means 55 degrees Fahrenheit, 40 to 60 percent humidity, dark, with no vibration. There are also public wine storage facilities in almost every large metropolitan area which charge from fifty cents to more than $1 per case per year for humidity- and temperature-controlled storage. Make sure they will insure your wine against extended power failures.

You should keep a written cellar book (software is generally distrusted because it could be easier to fake entries) which includes copies of all purchase receipts and provenance records for all your purchases. Your records should include the storage conditions and snapshots of the wine in the storage facility.

When it comes time to sell, a written and photographic record of provenance is as good as it gets. In addition, if you buy wine from an individual either directly or via auction, you should expect a provenance that is provable, and the seller should transfer all the provenance records to you upon purchase.

These records are vital for insurance purposes as well. Most homeowners' policies do not cover wine, and most insurance carriers will not sell you a special rider to cover your collection. In addition, if you visualize this as a business and take the steps to structure your investments so that you can comply with IRS requirements, realize that residential insurance policies specifically exclude commercial property. For this reason, you'll want a special policy such as the one offered by Chubb, which start as low as 42 cents per $1,000 coverage. You can e-mail them at *wine-collect@chubb.com* for the nearest agent. They do not typically require appraisals, except for individual bottles valued at more than $10,000 each, and will cover wine stored at commercial facilities outside your home.

Now that you have found your wines and a nice home for them, all you need is patience, because wine appreciation is a long-term investment with anywhere from five to ten years required for a decent return. But remember, if you're really in this for love and not money, you need to trust your gut instincts. Why go through life regretting the fact that you had all that great wine and let it slip through your fingers instead of past your lips?

ELEVEN

Opening Your Own Wine Exchange

Buying wine, wine futures, and wine equities for their price appreciation can offer its own financial satisfaction. But only when you buy wine for your own appreciation—to drink—do you realize the pure sensory dividends that wine can yield.

First and foremost, wine is for drinking. It shouldn't be so expensive that you feel guilty having it every night with dinner, nor stored so far away that you can't easily lay hands and corkscrew on it. After all, if you want to get your healthy glass or three per day, wine drinking shouldn't be a hassle, but part of your everyday life.

That means assembling a collection of bottles you like to drink and that you feel go well with the type of food you cook and serve. For lack of a better term, I will call this a "cellar," even though the number of wine collections that are in actual cellars is minuscule.

Most people begin a cellar by accident. They accumulate a few bottles here and there until the jumble starts to commandeer the counter space and the broom closet. Perhaps they find a wine they like and buy two or three extras, and when those are consumed they are dismayed to find that there is no more to be had. This is when the light dawns and people start buying a case or more, both to assure supply and to take advantage of case discounts that can range from 10 to 25 percent. These become the "house" wines that get opened day after day, and the mainstay for parties and events.

If you find yourself in this situation, you'll need a place to put the stuff. If what you're buying is for drinking over the next year or two, then don't worry about temperature-controlled gadgets and systems. Instead, make space in a closet or kitchen cabinet inside your house or apartment. The space must be dark (light can actually damage wine), as vibration-free as possible (not next to the disposal motor or central heating fan), and as close to the interior of your living space as you can get, since exterior walls heat and cool faster and subject the wine to extreme temperature variations.

As a rule, if you are personally comfortable with the temperature in your home, your wine should be happy in its closet for a year or two. And because they're all hidden away, you can store the bottles in the cardboard cases they came in instead of expensive wooden or metal racks. Just rip off the top flaps and stack the cases on their sides; they can go up to three or four high without crushing the cases on the bottom.

Many wine lovers also accumulate bottles of the really good stuff—the Latour, an Arrowood Cabernet, or a Matanzas Creek Merlot—that they want to keep for a decade or more. Obviously these have to come out of the closet and into more pampered surroundings. But pampered need not mean any more expensive than a good used refrigerator. There are only two temperature control devices designed to maintain a constant temperature (55 degrees Fahrenheit is recommended) in the used fridge, and they are extremely hard to locate: the Wine-Stat costs $149 and is available from BH Enterprises, (800) 973-9707, *www.concentric.net/—winestat/index.html*. A competing product is the CellarSteward, which costs $189 and is available from the Wine Merchant, (919) 834-0250, *www.launchsite.com/PrecisionStorage/*.

Both Wine-Stat and CellarSteward have temperature sensors that sit inside the fridge (you just close the door on the wires, no need to drill holes). The temperature sensor wires lead to a control box into which you plug the refrigerator power cord. The control box is then plugged into the AC outlet and, in turn, provides power to the refrigerator when needed.

The issue of humidity for wine storage has as much to do with urban myth as it does reality. Common knowledge calls for storing wine on its side with the humidity in the fifty percent range. Both of these factors are reputed to keep corks from drying out and losing their seals. There is no scientific evidence that this is true. However, if you decide to rely upon an old refrigerator as a wine cellar, you can be on the safe side by turning off the frost-free feature since it removes humidity from the air. In addition, a tray of water, periodically replenished, should keep humidity fine if you live in a dry climate. Battery-powered temperature/humidity gauges can be bought at hardware stores for less than $35.

So now you have a space for wine, begging to be filled. You have a few bottles that are lonely and need company. Perhaps you already know what you like and will set about fulfilling the wine corollary to Parkinson's Law, namely that the amount of wine to be stored always expands to exceed the space available. You could add on to your storage space, but I've always found that throwing a party is a good method of bottle management.

If you're contemplating building a cellar, the next five years or so will be a fantastic time to buy wine for a drinking cellar, with prices falling for nearly every price point under $25 and for all but the very best over that price. There are indications that the Asian economic crisis and overstocked cellars may even cause the prices of very exclusive French First Growths to decline. The result will be the best wine for any given price point since the last oversupply years of the late 1980s and early 1990s.

What to buy, of course, seems to be the eternal problem, especially for people who haven't consumed enough wines yet to know their own preferences. Just as with the expensive First Growths, a great way to sample several wines is to invite friends over and have everyone bring a bottle of wine. You'll probably want to specify a price range and the type of wine, then sip away. There is no need to think of this as a "tasting": enjoy the wine with food, swirl and sniff, then swallow.

Don't obsess over stemware: one set of basic stemmed wineglasses will do just fine. Don't buy those tiny thimble things or the oversized globes that look like props from a *Lost in Space* episode. And if you pay more than two or three dollars per wineglass, you're probably wasting your money. Expensive glasses don't improve the taste, no matter how the snobs rhapsodize over them. Those pricy Riedel glasses, one for each wine varietal, are an affectation made more for conversation than for drinking wine. The company claims they make wines taste better, but I have never seen any credible evidence to verify that.

Open the bottles and set them on the coffee table, gather around and sip. If you want to turn up the stress level, you can find a lot of books that will describe how to hold a wine tasting, but I wouldn't bother. This is supposed to be fun, remember? All you need is a separate glass for each sample poured so that you can go back and compare one wine to another. And you'll want paper and pen so you can remember the wines you like best (and the location where they were purchased).

Your job is immensely simplified if you live in a large or medium-size city, because the wine will come to you in the form of tastings (many of them free) held by visiting winemakers and by the better local retailers. Sadly, political pressure and lavish campaign contributions from wholesalers and distributors have made such tastings illegal in many states.

If you're lucky enough to live in a state where wine is sold in supermarkets and discount stores, you'll usually find that competition keeps prices low and that there is a good selection. Unfortunately, antiquated laws keep many people from buying wine and food in the same place. Most states have wineries where you can sample and purchase their wares.

If your state allows you to receive wine shipments directly, I would highly recommend that you let an experienced sommelier select wine for you. Peter Granoff, the Master Sommelier at Virtual Vineyards (*www.virtualvin.com*) regularly assembles a mixed case of twelve different wines for less than $100. I have never known him to pick a bad wine. If your taste runs to the higher end, another Master Sommelier, Doug Frost, will recommend some very old ports, classified First Growths, and other rare and aged wines at Wine Society of the World (*www.winesociety.com*). Frost is one of only two people in the world ever to obtain *both* the coveted Master Sommelier (MS) and Master of Wine (MW) designations.

Some traditional retailers also offer the novice sampler very good wines at reasonable prices, like Best Cellars (New York City) and the California Wine Club (multiple locations in California), which provide fertile hunting and sipping.

Consumers who are dazzled by all the choices in the marketplace frequently look for any scrap of information to help stave off the terminal confusion that sends many lunging for the Snapple display. Often, good information will come from "shelf talkers"—those Post-It-size notes attached to the shelf that tells you the wine was rated highly by *Wine Spectator* or some other authority (Robert Parker, *Wine & Spirits*, and *Wine Enthusiast* being the other gold standards).

You'll also find many with foil stickers proclaiming that they have won a medal at this judging or another. Most medals should be disregarded. With a dozen or so notable exceptions (including the California State Fair, San Francisco County Fair, Sonoma County and Orange County fairs), most medals are irrelevant because they are awarded during poorly run competitions with inexperienced judges tasting too many wines. Others are simply run unethically; I have been a judge at competitions where the tasters were pressured to award more medals. On the other hand, I have also been on tasting panels like the San Francisco County Fair, where no pressure was exerted.

As a whole, the wine magazines do a better job of rating wines even though their methods have flaws as well. Wines tasted by a panel often turn out homogenized, average ratings. On the other hand, wines tasted by individuals tend to favor certain varietals and styles over others. Indeed, several scientific studies have found that wine ratings are statistically insignificant because of inconsistencies and enormous variation.

"Scoring wine quality is a clear example of a Catch-22 situation," said Ann Noble, professor at UC Davis and the inventor of the Wine Aroma Wheel, a widely used device that helps categorize specific flavors. "Quality cannot be evaluated consistently by different people and often cannot be evaluated reproducibly by individual judges. The most experienced, skilled, and sensitive of wine judges will have differences of opinion about wine quality."

These studies have found that numerical scores (usually on a 100-point scale) tend to imply a precision that does not exist. Despite this, wide differences in ratings are often helpful in determining relative quality: Wine A is better than Wine B is better than Wine C.

The *only* valid rule for selecting wine is: drink what you like. Your taste is genetically unique, and no one in the world has the right to contravene that. It's certainly possible to calibrate your tastes against an expert's. You may like Robert Parker's recommendations on Cabernets and not Chardonnays, or one Chardonnay style over another. If he consistently pans a style you prefer, simply use the information to know when he's picked a wine you like by the way he pans it. My advice is to find one source that rates a lot of the wines you enjoy and follow it, rather than spending all your time collating tastings on the same wine from multiple sources.

The main corollary from the One True Wine Rule is: never let someone make you feel guilty about your wine choice. Steven Tanzer is a wine writer of considerable talent, style, and intelligence. But I will forever be struck by a single line he wrote which, while witty and funny, exposed an underlying arrogance. A reader asked: "What is the correct temperature to serve white Zinfandel?" Tanzer replied: "There *is* no correct temperature to serve white Zinfandel." I know very erudite people with enviable collections of Classified First Growths all kept in two-thousand-square-foot, climate controlled, custom-made wine cellars that cost more than the median American house—who also like white Zinfandel.

If *you* like white Zinfandel, *drink it.*

All of this is simply to say that I cannot possibly tell you what to buy, wine by wine, bottle by bottle. However, I will try to give you a starting point for discovering your own taste preferences. But you'll have to stop reading about wine and start drinking the stuff.

Let's start by assembling a three-case (thirty-six-bottle) palate-testing cellar (with a three-bottle sparkling wine tasting thrown in, if you like) that should expose you to a wide variety of flavors and wines which are easily found in most areas. Open a bottle every night and share it at dinner with a friend or significant other, and you will accomplish three things: (1) get your healthy two glasses of wine, (2) find some wines you love, some you hate, and others that are

merely interesting, and (3) roughly thirty-six days after
you start, you'll have a better idea of which wines
you'd like to have a case or two in your drinking cellar.
In urban areas and those states that allow direct shipping, you should be able to buy all thirty-six bottles for
about $300. In states like Kentucky, Florida, or Georgia,
where prices are artificially inflated by the wholesalers'
cartel, the same thirty-six bottles may cost you as much
as $400 to $500—if you can find them at all, since selections are also limited in these areas.

With all that said, here are my tasting cellar recommendations designed to expose your palate to the
broadest range of taste sensations while keeping your
costs down. There are a number of obvious omissions
here (Austrian reds and whites, for example), simply
because the wines are not readily available nor are they
usually found in the affordable categories.

Domestic Red Wine

1. Cabernet Sauvignon
2. Merlot
3. California Pinot Noir
4. Oregon Pinot Noir
5. Zinfandel (the original red version)
6. Petite Sirah
7. Sangiovese
8. Rhône-style blend

Domestic White Wine

1. Sauvignon Blanc
2. White Zinfandel (try it to say you've tried it)
3. Chardonnay

4. Pinot Gris
5. Riesling
6. Gewurztraminer
7. Chenin Blanc

In the import category, I have recommended ten whites and eleven reds. In many cases, the French wines that fit your under-$10 budget will be from negociants (people who buy bulk wine and blend it), but that's fine; there are many excellent wines here.

Import Reds

1. Bordeaux—Medoc (France)
2. Bordeaux—St. Emilion (France)
3. Burgundy (France)
4. Beaujolais (France)
5. Rhône (France)
6. Shiraz (Australia)
7. Italian Sangiovese (Italy)
8. Chianti (Italy)
9. Rioja (Spain)
10. Chilean Merlot (Chile)
11. Chilean Cabernet Sauvignon (Chile)

Import Whites

1. Alsatian Pinot Gris (France)
2. Sancerre (France)
3. Semillion/Chardonnay (Australia)
4. Pinot Grigio (Italy)
5. Macon Blanc (France)
6. Rhine or Mosel (Germany)

7. Alsatian Gewurztraminer (France)
8. Verdicchio (Italy)
9. Meursault (France)
10. Dry Rosé (Italy, Spain or Rhône)

Sparkling

1. French Champagne (aged *"sur lies,"* expect to pay $20 to $25 here)
2. California Methode Champenoise (pay about $10)
3. Charmat Bulk Method (pay no more than $4)

To truly sense the differences in taste and quality, I'd recommend that you save the sparkling wines for a weekend party and open them all at the same time to sample them side by side. Similar tasting event comparisons could be made by grouping the following wines together to compare styles:

- Burgundy, Beaujolais, and the domestic Pinot Noirs
- Italian and American Sangiovese, Chianti
- St. Emilion, American, and Chilean Merlots
- Pinot Grigio, American, and Alsatian Pinot Gris, Verdicchio
- White Zinfandel and European Rosé
- American and French Rhônes (add Zinfandel, Shiraz, and Petite Sirah for a larger tasting)
- Macon Blanc, Meursault, domestic Chardonnay and Semillion/Chardonnay
- Domestic and Alsatian Gewurztraminers, domestic Riesling, Mosel/Rhine
- Sancerre and domestic Sauvignon Blanc

- Bordeaux (Medoc), California and Chilean Cabernet Sauvignons (Rioja is its own grape, but you may want to throw it in here)

You may find that some of the reds, especially those from Italy and Spain, may have an "off" flavor right after the cork is pulled. These will often turn around in a matter of minutes when given an opportunity to breathe. But be aware that a wine will not breathe very well in the bottle since there is very little surface area for air to mix with the wine. So, instead of letting the wine suffocate in the bottle, pour it into a glass. In some cases you'll need to pour the wine vigorously (enough to produce some foam) to hyperventilate these wines into a pleasant state.

To see what the best minds in the wine field think of investments, wines, and winemakers, I surveyed a group of the most knowledgeable people who are in the business of serving consumers (as opposed to growing or making wine). The final group of respondees included six Masters of Wine, four Master Sommeliers, and one MS/MW. In addition, I had responses from four of America's top wine retailers and five wine managers at restaurants that have won every possible award for their wine lists. The questionnaire asked them to name five wines in each category (best to invest in, great everyday wines, conversation stoppers, etc.).

They are all very busy people, and generously spent a substantial amount of time responding to a fairly lengthy questionnaire. They were granted anonymity, since many of them are often in the position of selling wines that they honestly think are overrated, overpriced, or over-the-hill. There were many differing opinions, but I have taken the consensus replies and grouped them here.

Best Wines to Invest In

1. Don't invest in wine (most frequent answer)
2. Caymus Special Select
3. Prum Wehlener
4. Château Margaux
5. Grange
6. Château Leoville las Cases
7. True Vintage ports

Greatest Everyday Wines Under $7.50/bottle

1. Rosemont Shiraz
2. Laurel Glen negocianted reds
3. Fetzer Sundial Chardonnay
4. Farnese Montepulciano d'Abruzzo
5. Most Napa Ridge wines
6. Most Columbia Crest wines

Conversation Stoppers (Unusual Wines)

1. Any sparkling Shiraz
2. St. James Norton
3. Schug Valentine's Cuvée (sparkling Pinot Noir)
4. Vine Hill or Inniskillin ice wines

Most UNDER-Rated Wines or Wineries

1. Beringer
2. Shafer Hillside

3. Most great German estates
4. Swanson
5. Saintsbury
6. Arrowood
7. Kenwood
8. Lodi (California) Zinfandels
9. Sierra Foothills (California)

Most OVER-Rated or Overpriced Wines or Wineries

1. Domaine Romanée-Conti
2. Parker's favorite Burgundies
3. Caymus
4. Silver Oak
5. Heitz Martha's Vineyard
6. Hess Collection
7. Jordan
8. Opus One
9. Sassacaia
10. Dom Pérignon
11. Most Classified First Growth Bordeaux wines

Wineries on the Way UP

1. Schloss Lieser
2. Steele
3. Patz & Hall
4. Lewis Cellars
5. Harlan Estate
6. Niebaum-Coppola
7. Austrian red wines
8. McGuigan Brothers

Wineries on the Way DOWN

1. Sterling (and other Seagram wines)
2. Beaulieu Vineyards
3. Heitz
4. Jordan
5. Château St. Jean

And finally our experts offer two questions that the absolute novice can ask to tell if their sommelier/wine steward can be trusted:

1. Can you recommend a great bottle for $20 or under?
2. Why do you think this wine (recommended by the sommelier at any price) would be a good choice with our food selections?

TWELVE

Handicapping Wine Investments

IF ALL THIS WINE TASTING HAS WHETTED YOUR PALATE FOR even bigger investments, you can always call your stockbroker and buy a piece of a winery or vineyard. Today, average wine drinkers who've never been closer to a grape leaf than a plate of dolmas now have a wide array of wine, winery, and vineyard investments from which to choose.

Be aware, however, that the soundest of the investments are riskier than the average tech or industrial stock, without the same upside potential—and the riskiest seem to offer about the same odds as a state-run Lotto. This is not a warning to avoid these investments. People can and do make money. My caution, again, is to invest for the love, not the dividends (nonexistent) or the return on equity (average to poor).

While companies and market conditions change quickly, especially in the wine industry, there are some financial performance benchmarks that can help you sift through the choices to see if there are stocks you'd like to own.

The benchmarks come from examining the financial characteristics in best and worst performing wineries in a series of annual surveys conducted for more than a decade by the accounting and consulting firm of Deloitte & Touche, which has developed a respected expertise in the winery field.

According to D&T analyst Mike Rudy, who is in charge of the annual survey, the best performing wineries year after year met or bested most of the following benchmarks (see the appendix for information on the meaning of these ratios):

- Debt-to-Equity Ratio: 2:1   (lower=better)
- Fixed Asset Dollar   67%
  Investment: (lower=better)
- Current Asset Dollar   33%
  Investment: (higher=better)
- Asset Turnover: 1.0   (higher=better)
- Gross Margin: 50%   (higher=better)
- Selling Costs: 20%   (lower=better)
- G&A: 10%   (lower=better)
- Profit Margin: 18%   (higher=better)

Rudy found that the Return on Equity (ROE) for the top performing wineries varied widely even among wineries of the same size:

CASE VOLUME	RANGE OF ROE
Under 50,000	24-103%
51,000-100,000	29-173%

CASE VOLUME	RANGE OF ROE
101,000-250,000	36-39%
251,000-1 million	27-40%
Over 1 million	37-41%

Most of the wineries in the Deloitte & Touche survey are private companies. The reality for public winery stocks is that ROEs rarely attain 20 percent; 8 or 10 percent is more the average, and a significant number of companies that are publicly traded (including Beringer) lost money in 1997 and thus have a negative return on assets.

Finding most of this information is easy when you use Internet-based investment sites such as the Wall Street Research Network (*www.wsrn.com*) or StockSmart (*www.stocksmart.com*). You can type in a name or ticker symbol and automatically get a display of ROE, debt-to-equity ratio, and profit margin, as well as some other helpful ratios such as:

- Return on Assets
- Interest Coverage ratio
- Liquidity Ratio
- Price/Earnings ratio

To calculate all of the ratios, however, you will need to examine the company's filings with the Securities and Exchange Commission, namely the 10-Q quarterly filings and 10-K annual reports. Most of these are available online as well at one of two Edgar sites, a free one run by the SEC (*http://www.sec.gov/edgarhp.htm*) and a commercial one available by subscription only at *http://www.edgar-online.com/*. The SEC site does not always have all of the filings, nor do their older filings go back as far as the commercial site does.

A handful of wine and wine-related companies whose stock is traded over the counter (OTC) are not required to file with the SEC. You'll need to contact these companies directly for financial information. Any reputable company will send it out immediately.

Armed with your ratios and caveats, the time has come to survey the landscape to see which horses out there you can actually place a bet on. The public stocks we have picked for inclusion in this chapter are all traded on U.S. exchanges.

Agritope [NASDAQ: AGTO]   Rootstock produced by their Vinifera division.

Allied-Domecq [OTCBB:ALDCY]   Owns Wine Alliance; global corporation in food and spirits.

✓Andretti Wine Group [OTCBB: VINE]   All wine.

Araldica [OTCBB: AWLT]   Negocianted wines labeled with Italian family names, also sells cheese and specialty foods.

✓Beringer [NASDAQ: BERW]   Wine only.

Brown-Forman [NYSE: BFB]   Owns Fetzer and other wine brands. Primarily a spirits company which also owns some luxury goods companies.

Canandaigua Brands [NASDAQ: CBRNA]   Beer, wine, and spirits.

✓Chalone [NASDAQ: CHLN]   Wine only.

Diageo [NYSE: DEO]   Owns Heublein, Beaulieu Vineyards; global corporation in food and spirits.

Fortune Brands [NYSE: FO]   Consumer goods company owns Geyser Peak Winery, Jim Beam Bourbon, Master Locks, golf equipment, and kitchen cabinets.

Geerlings & Wade [NASDAQ: GEER]   Mail order catalogue retail sales of wine.

Golden State Vintners [NASDAQ: VINT]   Producer of

value-priced wines from Central Valley grapes with contracts to make wine for major companies such as Beringer and Mondavi.

Louis Vuitton Moët Hennessy [NASDAQ: LVMHY]   Champagne, luxury and leather goods.

✓Robert Mondavi [NASDAQ: MOND]   All wine.

New World Wine Group [OTCBB: CORK]   Owns Rivendell Winery of New York, wine publications.

✓R.H. Phillips [NASDAQ: RHPS]   All wine.

Scheid Vineyards [NASDAQ: SVIN]   Owns and operates wine grape vineyards, began producing wine in 1997.

Seagram [NYSE: VO]   Mostly entertainment and spirits. Owns Sterling, Monterey Vineyards, Mumm Napa Valley, B&G in France.

Todhunter [AMEX: THT]   Bulk and fortified wines.

U.S. Tobacco [NYSE: UST]   Mostly tobacco products. Owns Stimson Lane Wine & Spirits (Chateau Ste. Michelle, Columbia Crest).

Vina Concha y Toro [NYSE: VCO]   All wine.

✓Willamette Valley Vineyards [NASDAQ: WVVI]   All wine.

Four of these companies (ALDCY, DEO, LVMHY, and VCO) trade in the United States as ADRs (American Depository Receipts). An ADR is a U.S. security that represents a certain number of actual shares of the corporation whose stock certificates have been deposited with an American fiduciary (the Bank of New York is the largest, representing more than half of all ADRs). An ADR may represent multiple shares of a foreign stock or a fractional share, depending on how the company wishes to price it for the American market. In essence, an ADR is a convenient way for Americans to trade shares of a foreign company, but it's done in dollar amounts on an American exchange.

Before we investigate each of the public companies, it is helpful to see where they fit in relation to the American wine industry as a whole:

- Among all U.S. wineries, it's the Top Ten and everybody else.
- Among the Top Ten wineries, it's the Big Three (Gallo, Canandaigua, and Wine Group) and everybody else.
- Among the Big Three wineries, it's Gallo and everybody else.

According to Gomberg, Fredrikson & Associates, the premier statistical and research organization for the wine industry, Gallo produces more wine than the other two of the Big Three; the Big Three produce twice as much wine as the rest of the Top Ten; and the Top Ten produce 82 percent of California wine. Looking at it another way, more than 750 California wineries have to fight among themselves for crumbs: the 9.7 percent left over after the top 25 wineries have eaten their share.

A parallel situation exists nationwide, where some 800 non-California wineries produce the 10 percent of domestic wine not produced in California. You can see that this severely restricts the number of American wineries with sufficient resources to be good public company material.

The Big Three dominate the top of the market and are primarily producers of boxed, bulk, jug, and fortified wines. Gallo is quite capable of producing respectable wines, but most of its revenues are still outside the premium categories.

The Big Three

WINERY	MARKET SHARE (OF BIG THREE)	CASES SHIPPED
Gallo	56%	59.0 million
Canandaigua	24	24.9
Wine Group	20	20.9
	100%	104.8 million

Combined, these three powerhouses ship just under 61 percent of all California wine; Gallo alone ships 34 percent of all California wine.

The Seven Largest Premium Wine Producers

WINERY	CASES SHIPPED
Sutter Home	7.40 million
Mondavi	6.70
Sebastiani	6.69
Beringer	5.60
Heublein	5.35
Fetzer	2.97
Kendall-Jackson	2.55
	37.26

Collectively, the seven largest premium wineries produce only 21.6 percent of California wine, making them about two-thirds the size of Gallo. Significantly, while this group reported record profits and revenue growth for 1997, case volume increased by a mere 1.26 million over 1996, a paltry 3.3 percent.

The list of California's twenty-five top wineries gives you an even wider view. Those that are public or part of a public company are **in boldface** and have their trading symbol posted in brackets. For perspective, I have added public companies traded in the United States but located outside of California. These are in boldface and marked with a bullet instead of a number.

The Top 25 California Wineries

WINERY	PERCENT CALIF.	MILLION CASES/ WINE 1997
1. Gallo (wine only)	34.2%	59.0
2. **Canandaigua West [CBRNA]**	**14.4%**	**24.9 (~28.0 total U.S.)**
• **Louis Vuitton Moët Hennessy [LVMHY]**		**25.0 (worldwide)**
3. The Wine Group	12.1%	20.9
• **Vina Concha y Toro [VCO]**		**(worldwide)**
4. Sutter Home	4.3%	7.4
5. **Mondavi [MOND]**	**3.9%**	**6.7**
6. Sebastiani	3.9%	6.69
7. **Beringer [BERW]**	**3.2%**	**5.6**
8. **Heublein/IDV (Diageo) [DEO]**	**3.1%**	**5.35**
9. **Fetzer (Brown-Forman) [BFB]**	**1.7%**	**2.97**
10. Kendall-Jackson	1.5%	2.55
11. Golden State Vintners	1.3%	2.25
12. Bronco	1.2	2.1
• **Stimson Lane [UST]**		**2.0**
13. Delicato	1.0%	1.16
14. Korbel	0.7	1.16
15. **Wine Alliance [ALDCY]**	**0.7%**	**1.13**
16. C. Mondavi/Charles Krug	0.6%	0.97
17. **Beaulieu Vineyards [DEO]**	**0.4%**	**0.76**
18. **Monterey Vineyard [VO]**	**0.4%**	**0.65**
19. ASV Wines	0.3%	0.56

WINERY	PERCENT CALIF.	MILLION CASES/ WINE 1997
20. Domaine Chandon [LVMHY]	0.3%	0.46
21. Geyser Peak [FO]	0.3%	0.44
22. San Antonio/Maddelena	0.2%	0.382
23. Buena Vista Carneros	0.2%	0.38
24. Phillips [RHPS]	0.2%	0.372
25. Round Hill	0.2%	0.37
	90.3%	155.69
All Other California Wineries	9.7%	16.69
Total California	100%	172.38

As this chapter was being finished in late summer 1998, the headlines were filled with gushing news about how the California wine industry made record profits in 1997, an 11 percent increase to $5.9 billion. The stories—and the people selling wine stocks—glossed over the fact that consumption increased only 1 percent. Record profits are a house of cards if they are based on simply increasing prices rather than volume. Companies in this position are less likely to weather a period of oversupply than those who have increased both volume and prices.

To be sure, the oversupply was making itself felt early and often. By June 1998 wine prices in the $10 and under category had already started to drop as much as $2 per bottle, especially white wines. Red wines should see price drops starting later in 1998, with an accelerating rate of decline well into the next century.

The depression in prices is a result of the record 1997 harvest in California, along with ample supplies of good quality imports. In addition, the thousands of acres of new vineyards that should start producing commercial quantities by the year 2000 will keep shoving prices down. Between 1996 and 2000, the production of Chardonnay and Cabernet Sauvignon will have doubled in California, and Merlot will have tripled. While many of these grapes are from the Central Valley and destined for lower-priced wines, the price floor for all wine prices will still be lowered, making better and better wine available at every price point except for those ultrapremium wines that trade more on the basis of hype and investment potential.

Domestic overproduction also means that import brands will have to cut prices to compete or else face unsold inventories. All in all, the next five years will be great ones for wine consumers and pretty rocky ones for many in the industry.

As discussed earlier, grape costs can drop, but a winery's other fixed costs remain the same. On an $8 bottle of wine, a drastic crash in grape prices (let's assume 25 percent) saves an additional 25 cents per bottle over and above the existing 33 cents of profit, for a total of 58 cents profit. But the grape and wine oversupply, combined with stagnant or slow consumption rates such as those we have seen in the past decade, means the winery may have to cut its price per bottle by a dollar just to sell it—reducing the profit to just eight cents per bottle. In reality, an oversupply and the nearly 20 percent market share enjoyed by imports means a bottle that sold for $8 in 1997 may not move off the shelf until the price hits $6 or lower.

Wine and wine-related companies that are most likely to succeed in the coming period of oversupply and stagnant consumption are those:

- With large scale operations that provide an economy of scale and the best quantity discounts on everything from bottles to cork, grapes, wine, and other hard costs

- With relatively little debt. Even if official interest rates hold at their current level, lenders to the wine industry tell me that a downturn will present them with greater risks, and they can demand higher interest rates to justify the added risk
- Which concentrate their sales at the upper end of the price categories. An inexpensive bottle of wine has a very slim profit margin, and it is unlikely that any winery can increase volume fast enough to maintain current profits in an atmosphere of price cutting
- With a mix of nonwine products (beer, spirits, consumer goods) to help diversify profits
- Which own relatively few acres of vineyard, and have the resulting financial resources to modernize and weather the storm

But oversupply hits more than just wineries. Misery flows down the food chain. As you can see from the vineyard economic picture, a drop of 25 percent in grape prices (which the industry saw in its last oversupply period from 1989 to 1994) would mean financial disaster for many growers.

Especially hard hit would be growers:

- Who have borrowed heavily and have high interest expenses
- With small operations lacking economies of scale
- Without long-term contracts
- With older plantings and trellis systems that do not maximize tonnage produced per acre
- With Phylloxera-ravaged vines still to be replanted
- Without highly efficient farming practices, including mechanical picking, that can reduce farming, overhead, and harvest costs

Of course, growers with single-vineyard-designate wines and those going into $25 and up wines will be relatively insulated from the disaster.

All of this will put a greater focus on debt. Those growers and wineries that have relatively small interest expenses will be able to survive the coming lean period best. Any increase in interest rates or even a mild recession (which always decreases wine consumption) could put debt-heavy wineries and vineyards into a sale or bankruptcy position. It is not a coincidence that the last series of financially devastating years in the American wine industry—the late 1980s and early 1990s—were also years of oversupply. The only difference between 1990 and 2000 seems to be that today consumption is creeping up slowly. But the oversupply problem looks to be even larger in 2000; plus, the industry probably can't depend on a fortuitous fluke like the 1991 "60 Minutes" program to save its skin. Unless the industry reverses its decades-long habit of doing nothing to help increase consumption, the millennium is shaping up to be a Titanic year.

With all that in mind, the company briefings follow. It is impossible to give you an accurate picture of a company's revenues and financial outlook without citing specific numbers and SEC filings. I have tried to stay away from specifics and instead to focus on trends and fundamentals that are unlikely to change overnight. Specific financial figures will certainly have changed by the time this book is published.

Agritope (NASDAQ: AGTO)

While its main focus is genetically engineering fruits and vegetables, its subsidiary, Vinifera Inc., has staked its future on producing faster-growing, more disease-free wine grape rootstock. Agritope owns 61 percent of Vinifera, which is headquartered in Petaluma, California, in Sonoma County. It has propagation and production facilities there and in Woodburn, Oregon.

Through proprietary processes, Vinifera propagates and grafts grapevine plants for sale to vineyards and to growers of table grapes. Industry sources have estimated that 44 million grafted wine grapevine plants were produced in California in 1996. This number is expected to increase to between 70 million and 90 million by the year 2000.

Traditionally, grapevine plants for sale to vineyards are produced seasonally using field-grown, dormant cuttings. In contrast, Vinifera uses year-round greenhouse propagation and a herbaceous grafting method that employs very young, actively growing cuttings. As a result, Vinifera says it is able to develop about ten times as many new plants as can be produced with traditional techniques. In addition, herbaceous grafting with green cuttings could allow a newly planted vineyard to begin commercial production a year sooner than would otherwise be possible. This process also produces sturdier unions than dormant grafting, resulting in significantly higher yields of successful grafts, both at propagation and in the field.

The company's library of grapevine plants includes 32 different Phylloxera-resistant types of rootstock, 88 different wine varietal clones, and ten different table grape varietal clones. In addition, several French and Italian varietals are currently passing through quarantine and will be available to the U.S. market exclusively through Vinifera.

Vinifera believes that this collection of different grapevine clones is one of the largest in the world. Vinifera's U.S. customer base consists of more than eighty vineyards in California, Washington, and Oregon. In 1995, Vinifera established a joint venture in Argentina (Vinifera Sudamericana S.A.) to begin the propagation of plant material in that country. The first vines produced were sold in 1997. Vinifera is currently in the process of establishing similar ventures in other countries with large grape and wine production industries.

PROS:
- Black Goo, Pierce's Disease, and other grapevine pests should create demand for resistant vines.
- Faster propagation time than traditional methods.

CONS:
- Oversupply may decrease demand for new rootstock.
- Stock price has under-performed the S&P 500 Index since the company's IPO.
- No stockholder perquisite program.

PERQ RATING = 0

Allied-Domecq (OTCBB: ALDCY)

This $8 billion international spirits conglomerate also has interests in food (Baskin-Robbins, Dunkin' Donuts), restaurants, pubs, and wine.

Its main brands are Ballantine's, Teacher's and Laphroaig scotch (the latter being James Bond's choice), Beefeater Gin, Courvoisier cognac, Canadian Club, Sauza tequila, Kahlúa and Tia Maria, Presidente and Don Pedro brandies, Harvey's and La Ina sherries, Cockburn's ports, and Maker's Mark bourbon.

Allied-Domecq is also a major operator of food and drink retailers, with more than 4,000 pubs in the U.K. and 1,500 wine stores under the Victoria name.

The company's wine interests include:

- The Calvert Group, a large Burgundian and Bordelais negociant whose best known brand is Moreau Chablis
- The Wine Alliance in the United States, which includes: Callaway Vineyard and Winery, Clos du Bois, William Hill Winery, and Atlas Peak Winery
- Part ownership of China's Huadong Winery

The Wine Alliance says it sold more than one million cases of wine in 1997, the first year to reach that level. That puts its estimated sales revenues close to $45 million, a very small percentage of the overall company's gross. Company information does not list any wine brands as "main" brands, reflecting wine's minor financial position in the company.

Allied-Domecq has the most confusing and incomplete financial information of any of our wine stocks except for the three companies that have none at all (AWLT, CORK, VINE), and falls far short of the data provided by the other three international companies in our market basket that trade in the U.S. as ADRs (DEO, LVMHY, VCO). The annual report does not clearly separate revenues according to business unit and uses accounting categories that even the company's own investor relations personnel could not translate into the standard categories used in the United States. Finally, Allied-Domecq is the only publicly traded U.S. wine stock that is not electronically quoted, making it very difficult to get timely market prices.

The company sends its shareholders a booklet of vouchers that can be used for discounts on its products and meals. The calculated value (if all the vouchers are used) is in excess of $100.

PROS:
- Diverse mix of products and the relatively small size of the wine segment means that oversupply problems will not affect overall company performance.

CONS:
- Uncertain market position following the Diageo merger and the resulting strategic alliance with LVMHY. ALDCY board members have publicly discussed a merger with other drinks firms or spinning off the ice cream and doughnut business.
- Poor financial reporting and a scarcity of detailed financial information.

PERQ RATING = 5

Andretti Wine Group (OTCBB: VINE)

A small winery located just north of the town of Napa. Retired race car driver Mario Andretti serves as vice-chairman, and former Kmart chairman, president and CEO Joe Antonini is chairman. The company filed its initial public offering statement in March 1998.

Andretti has a forty-three-acre vineyard north of Napa planted with Merlot, Cabernet Sauvignon, Chardonnay, and Sauvignon Blanc. Twelve acres of the vineyard have been replanted and the rest is infested with Phylloxera and other vineyard pests. Part of the company's IPO proceeds was planned to be earmarked for this replanting.

The company filed its Initial Public Offering statement with the SEC on March 18, 1998, to register one million shares of Class A preferred stock and to sell 300,000 to 500,000 shares, the sale of which would raise between $3 and $5 million at an initial offering price of $10 per share.

The new preferred stock comes with no voting rights.

The company's existing common stock, currently traded in the Over the Counter Pink Sheets, has one vote per share.

Andretti has a winery with a 100,000-gallon per year production permit and a 6,000-square-foot hospitality center with a hard-to-obtain permit for a winery tasting room for public tours and tastings.

The company's wines sell in the $15 to $25 per bottle range; 7,300 cases were sold in 1997, up from 250 cases in 1996. The company said that it needs to sell 15,000 cases per year to break even.

The winery began in 1994 when two entrepreneurs licensed the Andretti name to produce, among other things, a wine commemorating the race car driver's retirement. The venture ran into financial trouble and on December 26, 1996, the founders' stock was purchased by Andretti and Antonini.

PROS:
- The Andretti name.
- Hard-to-obtain Napa Valley tasting room permit.

CONS:
- Winery is not profitable.
- Possible securities laws violations by previous management concerning $1.36 million in stock sales.
- At least three lawsuits which could materially affect the company.
- No written contracts with distributors.
- Company estimate of $11,200/acre to replant vineyards is more than $5,000 less than usual industry estimates.
- Twenty-five percent of sales are through one retailer, Trader Joe's.
- No formal contract with its consultant winemaker, Robert Pepi, Jr.
- High debt load.

- The company's accounting firm, Deloitte & Touche, attached the following warning to their audit of the firm's financials:

"The company has a working capital deficiency and limited capital resources, has had negative cash flow from operations and is having difficulty sustaining its operations and meeting its obligations as they come due. . . . The circumstances raise substantial doubt about the company's ability to continue as a going concern."

PERQ RATING = 0

Araldica Wineries, Ltd. (OTCBB: AWLT)

Headquartered in New Rochelle, New York, Araldica direct-markets Italian wines to Italian-American customers with bottles bearing the crest of their family names. It also imports wine from Italy, and markets cheese, olive oil, and other gourmet foods.

An investigation by *Wine Investment News* in August 1998 (as part of the research for this book) revealed that Araldica does not seem to have had a license to sell wine legally during most of the company's existence, may not currently have such a license, and further, that company president Frank J. Landi, Sr., was convicted of fraud in 1983 in connection with a company called Com/Link and served almost five years in federal prison. The details can be found in the Araldica pages at: *www.wineinvestmentnews.com*

PROS:
- None.

CONS:
- Questionable financial statements and no public filings.

PERQ RATING = 0

Beringer Wine Estates (NASDAQ: BERW)

This is the oldest continuously operating winery in the United States, founded by the Beringer brothers in 1876. The winery is well known for numerous *Wine Spectator* awards for "Best Wine of the Year," bestowed on the company's pricey ($45 and up) Private Reserve Cabernet Sauvignon. Beringer is also dominant in supermarket sales of White Zinfandel, which accounted for 40.4 percent of the company's 1997 net revenues, with Chardonnay bringing in another 26.2 percent and Cabernet Sauvignon another 10.9 percent. The Chardonnay and Cabernet Sauvignon fetching the most revenues are largely from the Napa Ridge line of wines, which sell for less than $10 per bottle.

The company's first quarterly filing in 1997 showed that its average selling price of a twelve-bottle case of wine was $51.42. Assuming that a case doubles in price by the time it gets to retail, the average case will sell for about $103, or $8.58 per bottle, which is Napa Ridge territory. Obviously there is a lot of White Zinfandel underselling this, and a little of the ultrapremium to balance things out. However, the relatively low per-case price means that the company depends heavily on lower-priced wines—precisely the wines whose price points will be most affected by a grape oversupply.

BERW also produces wine under the Meridian, Château Souverain, Château St. Jean, Stags' Leap, and Napa Ridge labels. In addition, it imports and distributes a number of prominent import brands including Gabbiano (number two market share of all by-bottle Chianti sold in U.S. food stores), Campanile (Italy), Tarapaca (Chile), and Rivefort (France). Imports make up about 4 percent of revenues.

For most of the twentieth century, Beringer was just another historic California winery making forgettable wine. That changed when the company was purchased by Nestlé in 1971. The winery improved greatly, but did not begin its meteoric ascendance until current president Walt Klenz was appointed in 1978. On January 1, 1996, an investment group headed by Silverado Partners and the Texas Pacific Group bought Beringer from Nestlé and then took the company public on Nov. 3, 1997.

The buyout left Beringer with a staggering $319 million in long-term debt, which gives it the highest debt-to-equity ratio in the wine business at more than 4:1. Their interest expenses were more than $26 million in 1997. By contrast, the Robert Mondavi Winery, which has roughly the same annual revenues, pays about $10 to $12 million per year in interest. And while some of the proceeds of the public offering have been used to reduce debt, the company is still paying almost $6 million per quarter in interest expenses.

The continuing presence of all that debt, and the company's own statement in its prospectus that the IPO would not give the company sufficient long-term resources and that additional capital would be needed, raises a question about all the vineyard land the company owns and whether it really makes financial sense.

Beringer ranks among the very largest vineyard owners in California, owning or controlling through long-term leases 13,659 acres in Napa, Sonoma, Lake, Santa Barbara, and San Luis Obispo counties in California; of these, approximately 9,400 are plantable. This allows it to fill about 48 percent of its grape requirements with grapes grown on its owned or controlled vineyards. On the other hand, Beringer says it buys more than 98 percent of its White Zinfandel wine from outside sources, thus putting its number one revenue winner at the mercy of the bulk wine market.

PROS:
- The stock has outperformed the S&P 500 index.
- A buttoned-down management structure which is probably the best in the American wine industry, headed by president Walt Klenz, who has served with the company for nineteen years.
- Profits are coming from both volume and price increases.
- Solid market share.
- Enlightened marketing and promotional philosophy.
- Products that encompass every price category.
- A solid strategy to counter import competition.
- A degree of financial sophistication unsurpassed by even the biggest Fortune 500 companies.

CONS:
- Heavy interest expenses.
- Market dominance, which can cut both ways. Beringer points out in the risks section of its prospectus that changing consumer tastes could hurt the company since 78 percent of the company's wine sales are concentrated in just three varietals: White Zinfandel, Chardonnay, and Cabernet Sauvignon.
- Large vineyard holdings, which do not represent the best use of capital.
- Phylloxera: Beringer's IPO filing said that as of June 30, 1997, it had already replanted 1,393 acres at a cost of approximately $20 million, and must replant another 1,026 acres over the next four years. At the same cost per replanted acre ($15,376), this will require almost $16 million. It is also betting that the sandy soil of its Santa Barbara vineyards will stymie

the pest. These have not been safe bets for other vineyards in that area.

• In addition to the Phylloxera replanting, the company said it was planning to spend "the majority of approximately $45 million" on vineyard acquisition and development.

• No shareholder perquisite program.

PERQ RATING = 0

Brown-Forman Corporation (NYSE: BFA, BFB)

Brown-Forman seems as conservatively solid as its best-known brand, Jack Daniel's. This $1.8 billion (1997 sales) family-controlled company's diversification from its Kentucky bourbon roots into leather (Hartmann Luggage), china (Lenox), flatware (Gorham), and wine (Fetzer and Bolla) makes it a sort of Louis Vuitton Moët Hennessy for the average American consumer. Like LVMH, Brown-Forman has a long record of paying dividends, and over the past years has slightly underperformed the S&P 500 (although doing better than LVMH).

This is primarily a spirits company, with other such well-known brands as Southern Comfort, Canadian Mist, and Early Times. It also has a thriving sales and distribution operation, which includes Korbel sparkling wines and brandy (worldwide), and U.S rights to Finlandia vodka, Bushmills Irish whiskey, Noilly Prat vermouth, Fontana Candida, and Fontanafredda Italian wines, Michel Picard French wines, Usher's scotch and Glenmorangie single malts.

Fetzer Vineyards is Brown-Forman's most prominent wine brand, best known for its affordable Sundial Chardonnay and its Bel Arbors "second label" of popular premium wines, which are now bottled in America with Chilean wines. The company also owns the Italian Bolla winery, most famous for its Soave white wine.

According to Brown-Forman's public filings, $1.3 billion (72 percent) of its 1997 revenues came from the spirits and wine operation. The company does not break out the wine revenues separately, but Fetzers's 1997 case shipments of almost 3 million cases at an estimated average wholesale price of $40 would yield revenues of about $120 million. The rest of its wine operations probably do not push that total over $150 million, so wine is probably no more than 11 or 12 percent of the wines and spirits segment and about 8 percent of total revenues. This stock is unlikely to see any substantial effects from the American oversupply problem.

While Fetzer is the ninth largest California winery, its relatively minor position in Brown-Forman illustrates the relatively small nature of the wine business compared with other industry segments, either in this particular company or in the economy as a whole.

The company was founded in 1870 by George Garvin Brown; the Brown family and related persons control the company by holding most of the Class A stock, which has voting rights, as opposed to the Class B, which has no voting rights.

PROS:
- Diversified business, relatively small wine portfolio.
- Consistent history of dividends.
- Solid, conservative management.
- Gross profits expanding faster than sales, which indicates efficiencies and tight control of expenses.
- Very low debt level (debt to equity ratio of 0.09).

CONS:
- Spirits are a favorite neo-dry target.

- Debt level so low that some analysts wonder if the stock might not perform better if it financed some expansion activities.

PERQ RATING = 0

Canandaigua Brands (NASDAQ: CBRNA)

Canandaigua is the second largest wine producer in the United States and also sells beer, spirits, and grape juice concentrate used for sweeteners in food and beverages. It produces, sells, or imports more than 125 brands, including:

- Wines (owned): Inglenook, Almaden, Paul Masson, Taylor California Cellars, Cribari, Manischewitz, Deer Valley, Dunnewood, Cook's, Great Western, Richard's Wild Irish Rose, Cisco
- Beers (import rights): Corona, St. Pauli Girl, Modelo, Pacifico, and Tsingtao
- Spirits (owned): Fleischmann's, Barton, Mr. Boston

Canandaigua is the largest grape juice concentrate manufacturer in the country, producing 12.2 million gallons in its 1997 fiscal year. And while it produces more wine than any other U.S.–based public company, its future looks increasingly like beer—and spirits, to a lesser extent—will be driving most of its growth and profits.

The company's fiscal 1997 annual report shows beer growing at the rate of 24.7 percent in dollar sales and 23.3 percent in volume over 1996, while overall wine sales inched up 2.5 percent on a 3 percent decrease in volume. While Canandaigua's varietal wines performed better— revenues increased 13.6 percent on a 2.9 percent volume increase—wine does not look like a long-term consistent gainer.

Indeed, the company's 1997 name and stock ticker changes (to Canandaigua Brands from Canandaigua Wine Company, and ticker to CBRNA from WINEA) reflects a reality that runs deeper than cosmetic appearances. All of Canandaigua's wines fit into the jug categories or in the lowest price segments of the popular premium category. For this reason, they will be substantially impacted by the downward price pressures of the domestic oversupply situation.

The company has two classes of common stock, with Class A having one vote per share and Class B ten votes. The Class B stock is not widely traded and is the method by which the Sands family retains control of the company.

PROS:
- Has outperformed the S&P 500 Index over the past year.
- Beer business is soaring.
- The company does not own a significant amount of vineyards.

CONS:
- Lower priced wines mean downward pressure on prices from oversupply.
- Grape concentrate business is very volatile and subject to international agricultural and weather conditions.
- Cisco and Richards Wild Irish Rose are "street" wines that come in for special attention by neo-Prohibitionists and government regulators.
- Import agreements for Corona and other Mexican beers (70 percent of beer sales) come up for renewal in 2006.
- No shareholder perquisite program.

PERQ RATING = 0

Chalone Wine Group (NASDAQ: CHLN)

This is the original wine-only public stock play, and remains the ultimate portfolio purchase for investors whose primary interest in wine is the love and not the money. The Napa-based company:

- Owns and operates four wineries in California: Chalone Vineyard, Monterey County; Acacia Winery, on the Napa side of the Carneros region; Carmenet Vineyard in Sonoma Valley; and Edna Valley Vineyard in San Luis Obispo County.
- Owns a 50.5 percent interest in Canoe Ridge Vineyard in Washington State.
- Owns 24.5 percent of Château Duhart-Milon, a classified fourth growth estate, the remaining 76.5 percent of which is owned by the Domaines Barons de Rothschild (Lafite). These are a distinctly different set of Baron Rothschilds than the Baron Philippe de Rothschild that has the joint ventures with Mondavi and Vina Concha y Toro.

Chalone went public in 1984 and created a shareholder-oriented wine and perquisite program designed for those who believe that dividends in fine wine are far better than pure financial return. There is no question that Chalone invented the perquisite program among wine-oriented stocks, and continues to keep that program head and shoulders above any other program in the industry.

Among the perquisites offered to holders of one hundred or more Chalone shares:

- The hands-down most extravagant shareholder luncheon held in conjunction with its annual meeting.

- Periodic shareholder dinners and events with Chalone management and other shareholders held at restaurants around the U.S.
- The use of winery entertainment facilities for private events.
- Substantial (25 percent or more) discounts on wine.
- The "Wine Library:" a glossy direct mail offering filled with an extensive list of wines, older vintages, shareholder-only wines, olive oil, and accessories.
- A "wine dividend" based on the number of shares held, which can be used for purchases from the Wine Library offerings.
- Package tours to wine regions of the world, including Bordeaux.

A check of wine prices from the Wine Library offering showed discounts of 25 to 50 percent compared against those offered by Internet and other retailers.

Equally attractive to its own wines are Chalone's allocations from the other properties owned by the Domaines Barons de Rothschild (Lafite) including: Château Lafite Rothschild, Château L'Evangile in Pomerol, and Château Rieussec in Sauternes. The Chalone Wine Library listed the 1994 Château Lafite Rothschild for $72 per bottle; the *Wine Spectator* listed it at $115 (and rated it a 93). Even discounters were selling it at more than $100. Likewise, the Duhart-Milon, which sells for $20.70 in the Wine Library, was going for $30 at normal retail. Applying the wine dividend (11 cents a share in the most recent full year) can reduce the price further.

Indeed, a hundred shares of Chalone stock could be quickly amortized in wine purchases alone. And this is a good thing because Chalone, which saw its best performance ever in 1997, has been a financially mar-

ginal operation since its inception, profitable some years
and not others. Its stock has consistently underperformed the S&P 500 index. The share price in early
April 1998 ($11.75) is not significantly higher than it
was a decade ago, when it was selling at $10. On the
other hand, your discount on a case of Château Lafite
alone could produce a return on investment that dwarfs
the capital gains on a hundred shares of the best performing wine or even technology stocks. The fact that
less than seven percent of the stock is held by institutions is a clear indication that this is a company for
individuals to invest in for the love of wine.

PROS:
- Treats shareholders like queens and kings.
- Offers attractive discounts on wine.

CONS:
- Relatively mediocre financial performance.
- Has underperformed the S&P 500 Index for the past
  year and overall since its IPO. However, it did
  mostly pace the S&P 500 from 1993 to 1997.

PERQ RATING = 10

Diageo (NYSE: DEO)

Diageo was formed in 1997 from the merger of two
British powerhouses—Grand Metropolitan and Guinness. The $23 billion company has substantial food
holdings, including such familiar brands as Burger
King, Häagen-Dazs, Pillsbury, and Green Giant.

Diageo's spirits and wine unit, United Distillers and
Vintners (UDV), was formed from Grand Met's old International Distillers and Vintners, which included the
old Heublein operations, and the United Distillers unit

of Guinness. The combined UDV sells more than 150 brands of spirits and wine in more than two hundred countries worldwide. More than 80 percent of UDVs revenues come from spirits, including Johnnie Walker, J&B, Smirnoff, Gilbey's, Tanqueray, Gordon's, José Cuervo, and Bailey's Irish Cream.

UDV's wine brands include Glen Ellen, Beaulieu Vineyards, Blossom Hill, Cinzano wines and vermouth, Le Piat d'Or, Croft sherries and ports. The company also owns 34 percent of Moët-Hennessy (a division of LVMH), which includes Moët & Chandon, Dom Pérignon, and Hennessy cognac.

No consolidated financial information was available as this chapter was being written, but an examination of the separate Guinness and Grand Met information indicates that for 1996, the most current fiscal year available, UDV's annual revenues were about $10.3 billion, composed of $5.73 billion from the old IDV, $3.97 billion from the old UD, and $650 million from the company's 34 percent share of Moët Hennessy.

This makes the UDV unit of Diageo the world's largest wine and spirits company. Indeed, the annual revenues of the whole company make it—all by itself— substantially larger than the entire American wine industry.

Diageo's wine segment, however, is an almost insignificant blip compared with the rest of the company. In the United States, the combined production of the old Heublein (encompassing mainly the Glen Ellen and Blossom Hill brands) and Beaulieu Vineyards comprised about six million cases in 1997, representing a 3.5 percent share of 1997 California shipments. While Grand Met's 1997 SEC filing claims that IDV had "in excess of 11 percent of the total domestic premium wine market in the United States," it's hard to see where the additional 7.5 percent could come from.

Based on the Heublein and Beaulieu Vineyards case shipments, their 1997 revenues were probably between $250 and $300 million, making them almost invisible in the overall corporate structure.

Reflecting this invisibility, Diageo's wine brands were completely absent from a large *Wall Street Journal* advertisement in 1997 announcing the merger and displaying the new company's key brands. In a key investors' brochure for the combined company, the UDV section does not mention any wines at all. Indeed, a letter circulated in early 1998 to key industry executives announcing that Diageo was preparing to separate all of the wine brands into a separate business unit, sparking speculation that it would put all its wine interests on the block.

This would not be the first time it has done this. In 1994 it sold its Inglenook and Almaden brands to Canandaigua. Until recently, the old Heublein had not had very good luck with wine acquisitions, gaining a reputation for buying brands, running them into the ground, and then selling them.

The Glen Ellen brand, purchased in 1994, has fared better. But excise tax receipts indicate that the Glen Ellen and Blossom Hill brands were stagnant in 1997, losing almost a full percent in volume, making its profits, instead, on higher prices—a trend that bodes ill for the company's sales in the coming period of oversupply.

Beaulieu Vineyard, by contrast, has begun a long road back toward its once-famous days of excellence. In a renaissance that began under president Richard Walton, the company has experienced double-digit sales volume gains. And even though the quality still falls a bit short of Napa Valley's best, it is on the increase.

PROS:
- Large international company with a diversified portfolio and substantial food holdings.
- Owns few vineyards.

CONS:
- Vast majority of wine volume (Glen Ellen and Blossom Hill) sell at the lowest end of the premium market, making them extremely vulnerable to oversupply price pressures.
- Stock has underperformed the S&P 500 Index.
- Uncertain commitment to wine.
- No shareholder perquisite program.

PERQ RATING = 0

Fortune Brands (NYSE: FO)

Entered the wine business in 1998, first in a deal to distribute Australia's McWilliam's wines in the U.S. and then in a big way with the $100 million purchase of Sonoma County's Geyser Peak Winery, which had revenues of $35 million in 1997 on sales of about 500,000 cases of wine. Geyser Peak wines include ultrapremium Geyser Peak Reserve and Venezia (more than $14 a bottle), superpremium ($7 to $14) Geyser Peak and Fox Ridge, and popular premium Canyon Road ($5 to $7 per bottle).

Fortune Brands owns the world's best-selling bourbon, Jim Beam, as well as a broad range of other distilled spirits such as Old Crow, Old Grand-Dad, Ronrico rum, Gilbey's gin and vodka, Kamchatka and Wolfschmidt vodkas, DeKuyper cordials, and scotches such as Whyte & Mackay. The company was formed in 1996 when the former American Brands divested its tobacco business, the American Tobacco Company. Distilled spirits make up approximately one-quarter of the company's $4.8 billion in 1997 revenues.

At its current level, wine, then, becomes a minuscule part of a consumer products company that also owns Moen faucets, Master locks, Day-Timers, and Swingline staplers, and major golf brands including Titleist, Cobra, and FootJoy.

Geyser Peak ranks twenty-first among California wineries and has 0.3 percent of the market, illustrating its relatively small nature compared with Fortune's other brands.

PROS:
- Diversified business, relatively small wine portfolio.
- Strong distribution experience with Jim Beam and other brands.
- Relatively small vineyard holdings.
- Solid, conservative management.

CONS:
- Spirits are a favorite neo-dry target.
- May still be a target of tobacco lawsuits and settlements.
- Stock has flirted with, but underperformed, S&P 500.
- Wine is a very small part of the company and may not get appropriate management attention.

PERQ RATING = 0

Geerlings & Wade, Inc. (NASDAQ: GEER)

Company markets wine and wine accessories directly to consumers in twenty-three states, where it is licensed or otherwise permitted to do business. GEER has almost 111,000 active customers.

The company said that in its goal of "reducing the intimidation factor" surrounding wines, it offers a relatively small number of wines and provides substantial information, tasting notes, and suggested food matches.

The company sources its wine mostly from small, lesser known European wineries and from the Codera Wine Group in California, a custom wine company that bottles wines under a variety of GEER's own brands, including: Glass Ridge, J. Krant Cellars, Hamilton Estates, and numerous others.

PROS:
- Company was profitable for first time in 1997.
- Has licenses and licensed premises and may legally ship to customers in a number of states that have fought most vigorously against direct shipping from outside their borders, including: Massachusetts, New York, Connecticut, Illinois, Florida, New Jersey, Washington, Virginia, Ohio, Minnesota, Colorado, and California. Its license in California allows it to take advantage of that state's reciprocal agreements with thirteen other states.
- Limited selection of wines helps control inventory costs and may help some consumers avoid being confused.

CONS:
- Company has been unprofitable until 1997; stock has consistently underperformed the S&P 500 Index.
- Has licenses and licensed premises in a number of states, which promotes an organization that must carry more inventory and hire more people than

would be necessary if the markets were free and the sales and shipments could be made from a central location. Geerlings & Wade is living proof that following all the rules, particularly in the punitively overregulated alcoholic beverage industry, is a shortcut to inefficiency and unreliable financial performance. They have done an excellent job of trying to follow all of the antiquated laws. In Massachusetts, for example, the company cannot give its members the same discounts as consumers in other states. In Massachusetts and New Jersey, GEER has to maintain its own fleet of delivery vehicles because those states will not allow UPS to deliver wine. These sorts of buggy-whip laws and GEER's compliance with them mean higher prices for consumers and/or a lower return to stockholders.

- Limited selection of wines narrows potential market.
- Most sales come as a result of direct mail solicitations, making postage increases a real threat to the bottom line. In addition, there are numerous documented cases where the U.S. Postal Service has thrown bulk mail into Dumpsters rather than deliver it. The most recent of these is the 1997 conviction of a postal worker in Gualala, California.
- Very slow entry into Internet sales.
- The company's marketing program seems stalled with few new ideas. Efforts to get affinity programs and other new initiatives off the ground have resulted in a lack of measurable progress. GEER hired a new marketing vice-president in late March 1998.
- No shareholder perquisite program.

PERQ RATING = 0

Golden State Vintners (NASDAQ: VINT)

One of the largest vertically integrated suppliers of premium bulk wines, wine processing and storage services,
wine grapes, and case goods in the United States. According to the Gomberg-Fredrikson report, GSV is the
eleventh largest California winery, producing 2.25 million cases of wine in 1997, giving it 1.2 percent of the
California market. GSV is a contract supplier for many
of the leading branded wineries in California because
of its reputation for quality and service, extensive vineyard holdings, strategically located facilities, and a full
range of products and services. GSV supplies premium
bulk wine under long-term supply agreements with
Sutter Home, Canandaigua, Sebastiani, Diageo, Vincor,
Mildara Blass, and other wineries.

The company also delivers contract wine processing, barrel fermentation, and storage services under
contracts with The Wine Group, Mondavi, Beringer,
and others. It also sells wine grapes, primarily to Gallo.
In addition, GSV produces private label case goods for
a number of clients, such as Archer Daniels Midland
Co., JC Boisset USA, and Trader Joe's.

Over the last five years, GSV has increased its revenues at a compounded annual rate of 19 percent, from
$47.0 million in fiscal 1993 to $95.8 million in fiscal 1997.

The company is the largest exporter of bulk wine
from California; in fiscal 1997, it derived approximately
12 percent of its revenues from the sale of bulk wine
and case goods outside the U.S. It is the second largest
brandy producer in the United States.

Golden State Vintners has 9,600 acres of vineyard
properties in Fresno, Madera, and Kern counties in California's San Joaquin Valley. There are 8,539 net acres

planted with French Colombard (35%) Zinfandel (14%), Chardonnay (13%), Ruby Cabernet (13%), Merlot (8%), and the remainder to other grape varieties such as Barbera, Carnelian, and Chenin Blanc. The vineyards produce an average of 8.8 tons per acre, and in the bumper 1997 harvest produced 10.4 tons per acre. The vineyards are almost 100-percent machine harvested, which results in greatly reduced labor costs. In addition, Golden State has production facilities in Fresno, Monterey, St. Helena, Cutler, and Reedly (brandy production).

GSV has established a reputation for the economical production of low-cost premium wines. In 1997, three of *Wine Spectator*'s top thirteen "Best Value" Chardonnays (under $10) were made with GSV wine. In addition, the company pioneered the use of inexpensive oak-assisted fermentation methods which have allowed wines such as its own Summerfield brand, which sells for about $6 per bottle, to be favorably rated with wines costing two or three times that amount.

PROS:
- Ability to economically produce value-priced wines for themselves and others offers the potential for better margins in times of tight supply, while also withstanding margin pressures in times of oversupply.
- Winemaking capacity is valuable resource in bumper-harvest years like 1997.

CONS:
- Highly concentrated winery customer base. Five customers accounted for more than 56 percent of the company's revenues in 1997. Gallo and IDV/Diageo accounted for 17.1 and 15.7 percent respectively.
- Highly concentrated grape sales customer base.

Grape sales account for about 17 percent of GSV's annual revenues, and of those, sales to Gallo were about 86 percent of the total. Equally significant is the GSV statement that they no longer have guaranteed purchase agreements with Gallo or any other customer, and as a result, "GSV will experience a significant decline in grape sales revenues" for the 1998 crop, which will be reflected in the company's 1999 fiscal year.

- Live-or-die dependence on Gallo. Combined wine and grapes sales to Gallo in 1997 accounted for 37.4 percent of GSV's total revenues, accounting for $30.38 million of the company's $95.78 million in revenues.
- GSV has 6,900 acres of vineyards, and, according to the company, "substantially all of the Company's vineyards are planted on their own rootstock that is not Phylloxera-resistant." GSV said that Phylloxera was discovered in its vineyards in 1997, but the hope is that the climate and soil in the San Joaquin Valley will slow the growth.
- Brandy sales account for 11.6 percent of revenues; brandy is a stagnant to declining product worldwide.

PERQ RATING = 0

LVMH Moët Hennessy Louis Vuitton
(NASDAQ: LVMHY)

An $8 billion luxury products powerhouse where haut couture meets haut wine. Its chichi brands include the widely counterfeited Louis Vuitton handbags and luggage, as well as other leather goods by Loewe and Celine, perfumes and cosmetics by Christian Dior, Givenchy, Kenzo, and Guerlein, jewelry by Fred, and designers including Givenchy, Kenzo, and Christian Lacroix.

The company also owns 61.25 percent of the DFS company, which operates luxury goods duty-free shopping stores, primarily in the Pacific Rim. This $2.5 billion purchase was made in 1997 just in time to suffer a tremendous hangover from the Asian economic crisis; Japanese tourists make up 70 percent of DFS customers.

LVMH's wines, spirits, and Champagnes (about 25 percent of the company's net sales) include some of the world's best known brands, including Dom Pérignon, Moët & Chandon, Veuve Clicquot, Pommery Ruinart Champagnes, and Hennessy cognac. It owns 50.66 percent of the ultimate dessert wine, Château d'Yquem.

In the United States, it owns Domaine Chandon (which produces sparkling wines in Napa Valley and in Australia), and 73 percent of both Simi Winery in Sonoma County and the New York import and distribution company Schieffelin & Somerset. It owns 73 percent of Widow Estates Ltd. of New Zealand, and 58 percent each of Cape Mentelle Vineyards of Australia and Cloudy Bay Vineyards of New Zealand.

In addition, LVMH owns approximately 11 percent of Diageo, with which it also has cross distribution arrangements. (Diageo in turn owns 34 percent of Moët Hennessy.) As part of these arrangements and in exchange for LVMH's agreement to accept the merger of Grand Met and Guinness, LVMH received $935 million from Guinness. In addition, LVMH has about $1 billion in postmerger capital gains from its investment in Guinness.

While sales of U.S. sparkling wines have been dismal for nearly a decade now—showing negative numbers or an occasional 1 percent gain—LVMH's

Champagne has been sold in record quantities, more than 21.3 million cases in 1996, for a 20.6 percent share of the entire Champagne market. In addition, the company's still and sparkling wine operations sold another 2.4 million cases that year. The 1997 revenues, released in March 1998, show a 32 percent increase in Champagne and wine sales over 1996.

These bright numbers have been somewhat offset by continued decreases in the cognac and spirits division of LVMH, down 13 percent in 1997 over 1996. The company has, however, made significant inroads in cognac sales to African-American consumers in the United States, which resulted in a 17 percent sales increase in 1997. LVMH has just begun a number of creative bar promotions in Japan targeting younger consumers there.

Despite sagging cognac sales and the Asian flu, which has afflicted the DFS subsidiary, LVMH reported a 23 percent increase in 1997 net income.

PROS:
- Diversified product line helps insulate against crashes in any single sector.
- Solid, top-of-the-line brands recognized worldwide.

CONS:
- Stock has dismally underperformed the S&P 500 Index.
- Lingering Asian crisis could continue to make DFS an albatross.
- Emphasis on luxury goods makes sales vulnerable to economic downturns.
- No shareholder perquisites program.
- Company is headquartered in France, which has an increasingly hostile attitude toward business.

PERQ RATING = 0

Robert Mondavi Winery (NASDAQ: MOND)

Mondavi is the quintessential California winery, the top brand in consumer awareness, and an institution that provided the spark that led California out of its jug wine mediocrity and into an era of world class dominance. It is hard to overestimate the value and contribution that Robert Mondavi—the man—has made to the industry as a whole, and Napa Valley in particular. His vision, energy, and success personify not just a winemaker, but an entrepreneur.

In addition to the original Napa Valley wines, the Robert Mondavi Winery (RMW) produces:

- Woodbridge, a popular premium wine (a segment also known as "fighting varietals," which retail for $4 to $7 per bottle)
- Coastal, (superpremium wine segment, $7 to $14 per bottle)
- Byron (ultrapremium wine segment, $14 to $20 per bottle and super ultrapremium, $20 per bottle and up)
- Vichon (bottled in the French Languedoc region, superpremium)
- La Famiglia (California-grown Italian varietals, ultrapremium)
- Opus One (joint venture with the Baron Philippe de Rothschild winery, super ultrapremium, more than $50)
- Luce (Italian joint venture with the Frescobaldi family, super ultrapremium, more than $50)
- Caliterra (Chilean joint venture with the Chadwick family, superpremium and ultrapremium wines)

The Robert Mondavi Winery owns 50 percent of Opus One, Luce, and Caliterra.

When RMW acquired nearby Vichon in 1985, it was a premium Napa Valley winery. In the following years, it drifted economically, not quite finding a consumer market or a niche within the other Mondavi brands. As a result, it was the obvious candidate for a change when RMW needed a new player: a brand that would tap into the ocean of wine being produced in the Languedoc region of France during the California wine shortage.

RMW made history in December 1996 when Vichon became the first California winery to relocate itself to a foreign country, attracting severe criticism from many others in the industry, who felt it would dilute the credibility and image of the California wine industry. The company had already taken criticism in 1996 it they started using Languedoc Merlot in the Woodbridge line.

This put it in the forefront of a controversy between California growers and their supporters (most visible of which is Sutter Home Winery), and a fairly broad spectrum of winery executives, including those at Beringer, Gallo, and Bronco, who realized that if American wineries didn't sell bottles containing imported wine during the shortage, then importers would sell the wine and gain an even greater market share. Wine had become a global commodity, and competition, they reasoned, meant thinking globally.

On the other end of the spectrum, Sutter Home bought a series of advertisements criticizing the foreign-wine-in-American-bottles movement and vowing to remain loyal to their growers even if it meant a loss to them. Such a stand did not seem to hurt the winery, which, according to insiders, increased wine case sales by 8 percent. However, as a private company, Sutter Home has the luxury of taking this sort of stand on principle, a choice that RMW does not have with a public market looking over its shoulders and expecting ever greater returns.

In this way, public offerings of larger wineries and the financial demands of the market will drive the globalization of wine and wine grapes. Whether they like it or not, growers and other wineries will have to deal with this fact or face being hammered, as were Detroit auto makers who didn't see the world economy coming to their neighborhood.

Whether Robert Mondavi—the winery—can maintain a position of leadership as a public company still remains to be seen. Robert's elder son, Michael, is the current president. He has managed the company during the best of times but is yet to be tested in a rough period such as the industry is likely to see in the coming oversupply shakeout.

The company's shareholder perquisite program— the "Partner's Circle"—includes wine and merchandise discounts, special and limited release wines, events, dinners, use of private dining rooms and facilities at the wineries, and a concierge service to help shareholders get the most from the benefits. Owners of as little as one share can participate.

PROS:
- Mondavi is the best-known premium American wine.
- Solid market share.
- Products that encompass every price category.
- A solid strategy to counter import competition.
- Relatively low debt level.
- One of the best shareholder perquisite programs.

CONS:
- Most profits have come from raising prices on almost flat volume.

- Overwhelming dependence on the Woodbridge line, which competes at the lower end of the price spectrum and will take severe downward price pressures in the coming oversupply. Woodbridge has become the inexpensively priced tail that now wags the Mondavi dog. According to a Smith Barney analyst's report, Woodbridge wines make up 77 percent of the company's case sales and 60 percent of revenues, with all other wines coming in as distant contenders. This dependence also has a tremendous effect on stock prices. MOND stock crashed twice in 1998 due to reported problems with Woodbridge wine supply and to market share decline.
- Overdependence on lower-priced imported wines, primarily Caliterra and Vichon, which accounted for 27.4 percent of the winery's sales volume growth in 1997. Margins on these wines will be depressed by the domestic oversupply.
- Large vineyard holdings (5,500 acres), which are not the best use of capital.
- Distribution is highly concentrated. Southern Wine and Spirits represents 30 percent of the company's revenues. Success by direct wine sales advocates could cause financial problems among wholesalers and distributors, which in turn could affect wineries that are overdependent on them.

PERQ RATING = 8

New World Wine Group (OTCBB: CORK)

Began life in 1996 as Rivendell Winery in the Hudson River Valley wine-producing region of New York state. It changed its name to New World Wine Group (NWWG) and its trading symbol to CORK on January

12, 1998. The name was changed after a limited partnership, Bayside Partners, purchased SmartWired, Inc., in November 1997, renamed it New World Wine Communications, and then sold 51 percent of it to NWWG.

The company does not yet make any formal filings with the SEC nor does it have audited financial information. Thus, most of what follows comes from company information and news releases.

Rivendell Winery was founded and is currently managed by two brothers, Robert and Fred Ransom. Located in New Paltz, New York, the winery produces mostly white wines: Chardonnay and the hybrid Seyval Blanc grape. The company also has a second label, Libertyville. Rivendell wines have been reviewed by both *Wine Spectator* and *Smart Wine* (which is now owned by NWWG). There are no current Rivendell releases reviewed by the *Spectator*, with 1990 being the most recent. Rivendell's very best 1990 Chardonnays rated a respectable 87. *Smart Wine's* ratings are more recent, the wine having been tasted in 1997. Those received mostly average ratings (74 to 81), and one, a 1993 Seyval Blanc blend white, scored an 87. This wine was actually produced for Rivendell by another New York winery, Vinecrest.

According to the Rivendell Winery Web site, it operates a café at the winery called "Café Noir," which offers its wine as well as "delicious platters of cheeses, smoked meats, patés, and other wine tasting fare." In addition, the winery has a wine of the month club operation called the Cellar Door Wine Society, and sponsors frequent events at the winery.

According to an online stock promotion site, *Market Pulse Journal* (which is paid by companies to create profiles that, in its own words, "informs and excites stock-brokers, investors, and shareholders through its sharp design and innovative format"), Rivendell Winery "is set to become the ultimate wine boutique." In the information, which was paid for and approved by the company before posting on the Web, Rivendell—now New World Wine Group—plans to:

- Create a showplace facility in New Paltz, N.Y.
- Acquire another New York winery
- Acquire (maybe a joint venture) a wholesale and importing company
- Begin a direct mail sales campaign using a mail order catalogue
- Use the Internet to "get the word out"
- Operate additional retail stores that would sell wine, food, and gifts, as well as operating restaurants and cafés

According to the NWWG-sponsored information on *Market Pulse Journal's* Web site, "Bob and Fred see the model of success with Starbucks and others like them, and they ask, why can't wine be marketed and its appeal be expanded in a similar fashion?"

Current and potential investors who have spoken to winery executives say they most frequently cite their aspiration to be "the Starbucks of wine" as the business area that holds the greatest future potential. The winery's Café Noir is cited as the prototype for the Starbucks-style chain. There is no current information from the company on the potential market for a chain of Café Noirs. By way of stockholder benefits, Rivendell Winery offers investors discounts on its wines.

PROS:
• Impossible to assess without proper information.
CONS:
• Impossible to assess without proper information.
PERQ RATING = 0

R.H. Phillips, Inc. (NASDAQ: RHPS)

Located in the Dunnigan Hills region about ten miles
northeast of the Napa Valley, R.H. Phillips specializes
in Chardonnay (47 percent of case sales), Sauvignon
Blanc (18 percent of sales), as well as Rhône-style wines
made from the Syrah and Viognier grapes.

The company has five brand groups:

• "EXP," a Syrah and Viognier, priced at $12
• "Toasted Head," named for the moderately toasted
  barrels, which includes a Chardonnay, and a Cabernet Sauvignon/Syrah blend, priced at $12
• "Barrel Cuvée," consisting of a 60 percent barrel-
  aged or fermented Chardonnay and a Cabernet Sauvignon, priced at $8 per bottle
• "Night Harvest" consists of three sweeter and fruit-
  ier wines—a White Zinfandel, a Sauvignon Blanc,
  and Mistura, which is a proprietary white blend—
  which are priced at $6 to $10 per bottle
• "Château St. Nicholas," a Chardonnay and a White
  Zinfandel sold only during the Christmas season and
  priced at $6 to $7 per bottle

Chardonnay accounted for 47 percent of the company's 1997 sales with Sauvignon Blanc coming in second at 18 percent. This is a smart cash flow strategy
for a small winery, since white varietals typically re-

quire less than half of the aging time than reds and can be sold quicker for faster revenues.

On the other hand, 85 percent of the company's sales come from its lowest priced brands (55 percent from Barrel Cuvée and 30 percent from Night Harvest), which will experience the greatest downward price pressures from the grape oversupply. The average selling price per case (primarily to wholesalers) was only $39.33, which does not leave much room for profit if prices drop.

In addition, the company owns or leases 1,549 acres—a very large number for a winery with net sales of $16.9 million and a production of only about 400,000 cases. On the positive side, the company conducted a sale/leaseback arrangement in 1997 with 371 acres, which freed up $5.38 million. In addition, the company said that only 187 acres of the vineyard is planted on rootstock vulnerable to Phylloxera.

Owners of a thousand or more shares of stock are eligible for 30 percent discounts on wine purchased directly from the winery, special shareholder bottlings, shareholder parties, tastings and events at the winery, as well as "Get Away Weekend" offers.

PROS:
- Shareholders get 30 percent discounts on wine.

CONS:
- Stock has underperformed the S&P 500 Index.
- Relatively substantial vineyard holdings.
- Price points of wine vulnerable to oversupply price pressures.
- High ante to participate in shareholder perquisites program. The 1,000-share minimum translates to a

$3,000 investment (at $3 per share), more than twice
the amount required for Chalone.

PERQ RATING = 7

Scheid Vineyards, Inc. (NASDAQ: SVIN)

The only public vineyard company in America, Scheid
makes most of its revenues from the sale of grapes from
its own vineyards or by managing vineyards for other
growers. It owns or manages more than 5,100 acres of
wine grapes in California's Monterey and San Benito
counties, two up-and-coming growing areas. Its customers and clients, most of whom have long-term contracts, include UDV, Canandaigua, Chalone, Morgan
Winery, and Gundlach Bundschu.

The long-term contracts generally require customers
to purchase almost all of the company's production at
a price based on the previous harvest year's sales
prices. The terms of these long-term contracts extend to
between 2001 and 2013. Contracts covering most of
SVIN's acreage extend to 2006 and have "evergreen"
renewal provisions whereby the contract continues
until either party gives two or three years' prior written
notice of termination.

Contract prices for SVIN's grapes are, on the whole,
at or somewhat above the average prices paid for
grapes in Monterey County.

1997 CRUSH REPORT, MONTEREY COUNTY ($/ton)

	RECEIVED BY SCHEID	MONTEREY COUNTY AVERAGE	SCHEID PREMIUM
Chardonnay	$1,572	$1,444	$128
Merlot	1,538	1,340	198

	RECEIVED BY SCHEID	MONTEREY COUNTY AVERAGE	SCHEID PREMIUM
Cabernet Sauvignon	1,577	1,115	462
Zinfandel	1,113	813	300
Sauvignon Blanc	1,031	943	88

SVIN has also started a winery that produced 4,000 cases of wine in 1997, most of it in the ultrapremium category priced from $18 to $22 per bottle. It sells wine under the Scheid Vineyards and San Lucas Vineyards labels.

Scheid says it has pioneered a number of modern techniques to increase the number of tons per acre without sacrificing quality, including new trellis systems and interplanting new vines in existing vineyards. Scheid says that doubling the number of vines per acre can increase yields by 60 percent without increasing farming costs by a comparable percentage. Only the future will tell if this will pay off, since the company's grape yields have been respectably average, as shown by the following chart calculated from public data:

	1993	1994	1995	1996	1997
Tons Per Acre	5.5	4.8	3.6	4.8	5.1

PROS:
- Relatively little debt.
- Most of its grapes are sold under long-term contracts.
- An efficient, well-managed operation with good

economies of scale, and seems to spend sufficient capital to keep its farming operations up to date.

- Has an active perquisite program for stockholders that includes discounts on wine and winery merchandise.
- The high percentage of the stock held by institutions (more than 81 percent) is a recognition of the company's solid management.

CONS:

- The high percentage of the stock held by institutions holds the possibility for wild price swings, since institutions tend to buy and sell stock in large amounts using computer program trading systems.
- In addition to all of the risks associated with agriculture of any kind, Scheid's relationship with UDV (which began in 1972) is something of a double-edged sword. With UDV accounting for about 81 percent of total revenues, according to SVIN's public filings, SVIN's future is joined at the hip with Diageo. While the long term and evergreen nature of the contracts offer some cushion, if Diageo acts suddenly and adversely, it will be a true test of management mettle for Scheid to replace that business with other customers, especially in an era of oversupply.
- The company's filings indicate that 76 percent of its acreage is planted or interplanted with Phylloxera-resistant rootstock, but that the remaining 763 net vine acres (land with vines, and excluding roads, etc.) are susceptible and may need replanting. At $18,000 per acre, this is a potential $13.7 million liability, which fortunately can be spread over several years.
- Finally, an oversupply of grapes will inevitably exert a downward pressure on SVIN's revenues and profits, either moderating increases or causing drops,

depending on the severity of the oversupply. Founder, chairman, and CEO Al Scheid told me that the company has never had an unprofitable year since its founding in 1977, even during previous periods of grape oversupply.

PERQ RATING = 5

Seagram Company Ltd. (NYSE: VO)

Seagram is in the business of entertainment (Universal Studios, Home Shopping Network, MCA and Polygram Records), spirits (Chivas Regal, Crown Royal, VO), and wine.

The company's main wine brands include, in the U.S., Sterling Vineyards, The Monterey Vineyard, Tessera Mumm Cuvée Napa sparkling wine; and in Europe, Barton & Guestier, Mumm and Perrier-Jouët Champagnes, and Sandeman ports and sherries. Seagram also imports and/or distributes a large number of brands, including Napa Valley's Dominus Estate, and the French classified growths of Château Lafite-Rothschild, Château Mouton Rothschild, Château Latour, Château Margaux, Château Haut-Brion, and Château Petrus.

While the vast majority of Seagram's alcoholic beverage revenues comes from spirits, it operates wineries and bottling facilities in twelve countries around the world. The company does not break out wine-related financial information, and thus it is impossible to precisely determine that percentage of its revenues.

However, of the $12.5 billion in revenues reported for its fiscal year ending June 30, 1997, the company said that $5.1 billion was attributed to spirits and wine. Industry sources and excise tax records show the total column sales of Seagram's U.S. wineries at something under 2 million cases per year, certainly less than an estimated $100 million. This would place its U.S. winery operations at about 2 percent of the overall spirits and wine revenues, less than one percent of the entire corporation's revenues. It is hard to see how even adding worldwide operations could top 5 percent and 2 percent respectively.

Sorting out wine revenues is doubly difficult because the company has two divisions that handle wine: the Seagram Spirits and Wine Group, headed by Steven J. Kalagher, who is also executive vice-president of the overall company; and the Seagram Château & Estate Wines Company, headed by Samuel Bronfman II, older brother of overall corporation president Edgar Bronfman, Jr. An uneasy relationship exists between the two wine-related divisions, both subsidiaries of Joseph E. Seagram & Sons, Inc., the overall company's U.S. subsidiary. Company sources say that the Seagram Spirits and Wine Group is primarily concerned with spirits and is thus the dominant operating unit of the company's worldwide alcoholic beverages operations.

According to a number of former company executives, the relatively small size of the wine operations has relegated them to somewhat of a stepchild within the organization, resulting in an inconsistent management strategy that has left doubts as to the company's commitment to its wine segment.

PROS:
- Wine is an almost negligible part of the overall operation, thus the company is unlikely to be substan-

tially impacted by the world oversupply of wine grapes.

CONS:

• Stock price has underperformed the S&P 500 Index.
• No shareholder perquisite program.
• Largest U.S. operation, The Monterey Vineyard, sells in the under-$10 per bottle range and will be impacted by oversupply, as will the Barton & Guestier wines.
• Questionable commitment to wine.

PERQ RATING = 0

Todhunter International, Inc. (AMEX: THT)

Produces distilled spirits, fortified wines, vinegar, cooking wine, and tax breaks. The company also does contract bottling for other companies, sells grain alcohol to Russian and East European producers of vodka, and industrial alcohol to hospitals, universities, and fragrance producers.

The Florida-based company distills its citrus brandy and spirits from citrus molasses, a byproduct of juice processing. Citrus wine is made from juice concentrate, then fortified to increase its alcohol content to approximately 20 percent, and sold to spirits and liqueur bottlers as a less expensive alternative to distilled alcohol. The company explains that federal excise taxes are $13.50 per proof gallon of distilled spirits (a proof gallon is about two and a half gallons of fortified citrus wine), but only $1.57 per gallon of wine.

By law, citrus wine can constitute up to 49 percent of the alcohol content of cordials and liqueurs, and up to about 10 percent of Canadian whiskey. In addition, smaller amounts of fortified citrus wine can be used in blended whiskey, rum, brandy, and other types of alcoholic beverages. The producers of these beverages can lower their excise tax bills substantially by substituting Todhunter's fortified citrus wine for distilled alcohol. In 1997, Todhunter sold 6.4 million gallons of fortified citrus wine and 11.3 million proof gallons of distilled products (citrus brandy, citrus and cane spirits, rum and grain alcohol). The Joseph E. Seagram Company (the U.S. subsidiary of the Canadian entertainment and spirits company) is a major customer, as are other well-known companies and brands.

Todhunter also produces rum, gin, vodka, tequila, cordials, and a range of whiskies for sale under its own proprietary labels ("James Harbor") and as private label brands for a number of retailers. Visitors to the U.S. Virgin Island of St. Croix (where Todhunter operates a rum distillery) will recognize the brand name Cruzan and some of the company's other rums, including Ron Carlos and Conch Republic.

Contract bottling of coolers, prepared cocktails, as well as nonalcoholic carbonated and noncarbonated beverages, vinegar, and cooking wine totaled 4.5 million cases for third parties and 1.3 million cases for itself in 1997. Its ten-million-case capacity means it has plenty of room for expansion. This excess capacity results, in part, from a drop of 32 percent in the contract bottling business in 1997 over 1996.

A major part of Todhunter's business is the production of a wide range of vinegars: red and white wine, balsamic, rice, corn, tarragon, and apple cider, which are sold in large quantities to manufacturers and distributors. This business grew 23 percent in 1997 and made up about 12 percent of the company's revenues.

PROS:

- No grape wine means it is totally unaffected by oversupply.
- Successful marketing efforts by large spirits companies to increase consumption would increase demand for the company's additive products and its case goods as well.

CONS:

- Revenues have shown a downward trend over past two years.
- No shareholder perquisite program.
- Distilled spirits are a favorite neo-Prohibitionist target.
- Closing of the wine vs. distilled spirits tax loophole could be disastrous.

PERQ RATING = 0

U.S. Tobacco (NYSE: UST)

Company derives 86 percent of its income from the sales of chewing tobacco, snuff, and cigars. It is also the owner of International Wine & Spirits, best known for its Château Ste. Michelle and Columbia Crest brands, which accounted for approximately 70 percent of wine revenues from the entire Washington wine industry. Château Ste. Michelle has played a key role in incubating the entire Washington wine industry and helping it to gain its international reputation. Its leadership and fostering of the industry is the best example of how a market leader can prosper as it helps develop the market as a whole. If Gallo had ever demonstrated even a fraction of the leadership exhibited by Stimson Lane Wine & Spirits (the American foundation of UST's wine business), the American wine industry—and

Gallo's revenues along with it—would probably be several times its current size. President Allen Shoup is probably one of the best two or three managers in the entire wine industry.

The company also owns two other brands, Villa Mt. Eden and Conn Creek, and is the importer and marketer of the French Colour Volant label. In addition, it owns and operates a craft brewery in Yakima, Washington, which produces the "Bert Grant" brand of ales and beers.

Château Ste. Michelle was created in 1967 by American Wine Growers, a winery that produced mostly sweet fortified wines. That year, legendary winemaker Andre Tchelistcheff (the man responsible for Beaulieu Vineyards' most memorable vintages) was hired as a consultant to get Ste. Michelle off to a premium start. The winery was bought by a group of investors in 1972 and sold to U.S. Tobacco in 1974.

Revenues from wine ($145 million) made up 10.3 percent of UST's 1997 sales, an increase of 18.4 percent over 1996. Total case volume was up 6.8 percent.

The wine segment of UST illustrates the asset and capital intensity of the wine business compared with the tobacco business. While the wine sector accounted for 10.3 percent of revenues, it only contributed 3.9 percent of the company's operating profit, while consuming 35 percent of capital expenditures and accounting for 26 percent of total assets.

Perhaps the best thing that could happen to International Wine & Spirits is a Beringer-style buyout with the extensive vineyard holdings spun off in a sale-leaseback arrangement. Increased taxes on tobacco, class action lawsuits, and other pressures may force UST to divest the wine operation to raise cash.

PROS:
- Well-managed.
- Top brands.
- Good market position.

CONS:
- Owns more than 21,000 acres of vineyards (3,390 planted) and other agricultural property, an asset drain and Phylloxera risk.
- Owned by a tobacco company.
- Columbia Crest brand, which constitutes most of the wine sector's sales, competes in the lower price ranges and should experience downward price pressures from grape oversupply.

PERQ RATING = 0

Vina Concha y Toro (NYSE: VCO)

The largest winery in Chile and the largest exporter of Chilean wine to the United States. Founded in 1883 by Don Melchor de Concha y Toro, the winery is to Chile what the Robert Mondavi Winery is to the United States. It is the country's best-known brand, an innovator in both vineyards and winemaking, and produces wine in every price category, from jug-type wines sold to the Chilean market in Tetra Brik boxes to the ultra-premium Don Melchor brand, which has consistently been highly rated by the top arbiters of wine quality. And in the same spirit as the Opus One Mondavi/Rothschild joint venture, VCO in 1996 signed a deal with the Baron Philippe de Rothschild winery to produce a limited production wine which will sell, like Opus, for more than $50.

With annual 1997 revenues of $144 million, it is almost half the size as the Robert Mondavi Winery.

PROS:
- Most of its wine (54 percent) is exported. It is the country's largest single exporter, exporting 20 percent of all Chilean wine.
- Extensive vineyard holdings (5,728 acres) allows it to control its grape supply.
- Offers the most thorough investor information of any ADR-traded foreign company, with extensive descriptions of its operations, financial information into U.S. dollars, and the conversion of selected numbers into those that comply with U.S. Generally Accepted Accounting Practices.

CONS:
- Shares have under-performed the S&P 500 Index.
- The United States is the largest single export market, representing 46.9 percent of all VCO exports; the American wine-grape oversupply will put downward pressure on VCO's wine prices, which increased 37.7 percent in 1997 on a 24 percent increase in volume.
- VCO relies on a single, exclusive U.S. distributor, Banfi Products Corporation, for all its U.S. sales. This concentration puts VCO at risk in the event that Banfi is unable to sell as aggressively, has financial problems of its own, or its management gets distracted by its own announced public offering on the Milan stock exchange.
- Vineyards are planted on the original vinifera rootstock varieties imported from France 120 years ago. There is no guarantee that strict import quarantine controls can continue to keep Phylloxera out of the country. Extensive vineyard holdings not only tie up capital, but leave VCO with a large exposure here.
- No shareholder perquisite program.

PERQ RATING = 0

Willamette Valley Vineyards Inc. (NASDAQ: WVVI)

This is the Rocky Horror Picture Show of public winery stocks: a cult phenomenon with its 3,600 shareholders who staff the tasting room and winery events, pick grapes, help out in the cellar, promote the brand to friends, restaurants, and stores, buy a lot of the wine to drink (in some cases at almost 50 percent off), and in recognition of their work, have their own personalized winery business cards.

"The company views its shareholders as an army of volunteer marketers," says winery chairman and president Jim Bernau.

WVVI is located just off Interstate 5 near Salem, Oregon, in the midst of the state's up-and-coming Burgundian-style wine movement. Accordingly, the winery in 1997 produced 91,700 cases of Pinot Noir (its largest selling varietal), Chardonnay, Pinot Gris, Riesling, Gewurztraminer, and a blush blend called Oregon Blossom.

WVVI is a "for love" investment, consistently among the three stocks that have performed worst against the S&P 500 Index than any other winery stocks (the other two in the cellar are Araldica and Geerlings & Wade). But capital gains are not what WVVI's investors are looking for. They want to be involved, to get their hands dirty in some part of the business, to be a part of the show . . . and to drink some pretty good Pinot Noir and other wines in the process.

Many of the stockholders are locals and other Oregonians who want to be part of this new "wine thing" where vineyards are filling up the cow pastures between the pear orchards, raspberry fields, and hazelnut groves.

In addition to admission to special winery events,

wine discounts, and priority for purchasing limited edition wines, the most valuable perquisite for shareholders is the privilege of sweating for their equity. Not surprisingly, institutions hold only 0.02 percent of the winery stock.

The winery certainly can use its shareholders' efforts to help stabilize the operation after a series of missteps in 1996 and 1997 that left the winery with more wine than it could sell and more production capacity than it needed. The company said that it had taken action to correct its flawed sales projection process, which had prompted it to produce excess inventory and, in part, prompted it to buy nearby Tualatin Vineyards for its production capacity.

If it can get its operational house in order, WVVI could be in a good position to capitalize on the state's growing wine industry, which is still minuscule by California standards. According to WVVI's estimates, the entire state produced about 760,000 cases of wine worth about $76 million at retail ($38 million at wholesale prices). The growing climate seems ideal for Burgundian varietals, as evidenced by scores of rave reviews for the area (and some for WVVI) from the top critics, including Robert Parker, *Wine Spectator*, and *Wine Enthusiast*. Vineyard land here is relatively inexpensive ($3,500 per acre, compared with $35,000 and higher in California). Climate and vineyard prices have prompted other well-known winemakers to begin developing Oregon properties. Those include: Burgundian negociant Robert Drouhin, Champagne house Taittinger, Sonoma Valley's Benziger family (which started the Glen Ellen brand before selling it to Heublein), and a number of Napa Valley vintners, including Girard, Stag's Leap, and Pine Ridge.

Also in WVVI's favor: Pinot Noir is one of the fastest growing wine varietals, showing annual increases in supermarket sales as high as 47 percent according to InfoScan.

PROS:
- Devoted stockholders.
- Unique shareholder perquisite program.
- Up and coming wine area and varietals.
- Relatively low debt.
- Major share of Oregon wine production.

CONS:
- Abysmal stock price performance.
- Management is learning the wine business "on the job."

PERQ RATING = 0

THIRTEEN

The REIT Stuff?

Concern over the capital tied up in vineyards has prompted many wineries to sell their vineyards to third party investment firms which then lease the grapes back on a long-term basis. But selling a vineyard to a third party does not make the land and the money tied up in it go away. In fact, it seems that the key players who have bought vineyards from wineries and leased them back intend to package those vineyards into Real Estate Investment Trusts.

Publicly traded Real Estate Investment Trusts (REITs) were hot securities through most of the 1990s, which is why almost every person who had bought wine country vineyard land as an investment (as opposed to a grower who does it for a living) spent a lot of time figuring out how to cash out. Problem is, vineyards and other agricultural land as a whole don't make for a very good REIT investment.

REITs were created by Congress in 1960 as a way for people of modest means to invest in real estate. The concept was for a well-financed company (a REIT) to buy income-producing properties and then allow individuals to buy shares in the REIT. To make the investments more attractive, Congress exempted REITs from corporate income taxes so long as they pay at least 95 percent of their taxable income as dividends to the shareholders.

The foundations of today's REITs are the gravestones of the REITs and real estate that crashed and burned in the late 1980s. Back then, speculators poured billions of dollars into the real estate market, much of it based on inflated appraisal values which lenders demanded to justify the loans that were made. When the real estate market crashed, the property landed in the laps of the financial institutions that had financed it, and when the S&Ls crashed and burned, in the hands of the federal Resolution Trust Corporation, the government agency charged with cleaning up the real estate disaster. The RTC then sold the property for pennies on the dollar, much of it to today's REITs, thus launching the REIT mania of the late 1990s.

A REIT revival was inevitable because creative securities dealers had turned nearly every other American asset into a publicly traded security by the end of the twentieth century. But by 1997, almost all of the $2 to $3 trillion worth of commercial real estate was in private hands: 93 percent of all apartment buildings, 95 percent of all industrial warehouses and light industrial parks, 96 percent of office buildings, and 78 percent of retail malls. Indeed, REITs as a whole began showing substandard returns in 1998. As acquisitions and growth stalled, many began to sell properties and take the profits to bolster their bottom lines. This factor and the concern expressed by the Federal Reserve about the level of REIT debt depressed stock prices of publicly traded REITs.

REITs started changing their own investment climate in mid-1995. By then the REITs that had been successful by bottom fishing for cheap and Chapter 11 properties left over from the real estate crash of the late 1980s had started to run out of purchase prospects. But heavy bidding for properties drives up the prices REITs must pay, resulting in a need for more new capital, thus beginning a vicious cycle that could result in an overheating of the market which could turn this boom into a bust.

Kurt Smith, director of real estate consulting for the Frank Russell Company, which advises pension plans, told the *New York Times* that he was concerned about the huge amount of money in REITs and real estate in general. "There's a risk with so much money flowing in," he said, adding that he was keeping an eye out for the return of "ego-driven trophy buyers."

Most experts agree that premium vineyards fit the trophy category.

The Prudential Insurance Company's August 20, 1998, sale of 2,500 acres of wine-grape vineyards in Sonoma, San Joaquin, and Sacramento counties launched a portfolio of trophy properties on the first stage of a path toward securitization. Real estate analysts are equivocal about its prospects. The purchase, the first for newly organized Silverado Premium Properties, of Napa, is estimated at $60 million by industry newsletter *Global Wine News*. The transaction is part of a continuing trend by Prudential, currently owned by policy holders, which has divested itself of more than $5 billion in real estate properties in preparation to go public.

While Silverado's lead investor is distressed-property-specialist Colony Capital of Los Angeles, the idea for the company was conceived by Napa Valley wheeler-dealers David Freed and former Beringer president Mike Moone, who were the masterminds of the leveraged buyout (along with the Texas-Pacific Group) that purchased Beringer Wine World from Nestlé and then took it public as Beringer Wine Estates Holdings.

Since 1991, Freed and his partners have established a near monopoly on the sale and lease-back of vineyards, which allows wineries to free up the capital tied up in the land—$35,000 to $50,000 per acre for a producing vineyard—while assuring its access to the grapes through long-term contracts.

Silverado's joined-at-the-hip relationship with Beringer also gives it first dibs on more than 2,000 acres of vineyards. Indeed, Beringer could use the cash from selling the vineyards to reduce debt left over from the leveraged buyout. Such a deal would certainly boost its stock price.

In 1997, Freed announced his intent to raise some $200 million in order to amass a portfolio of up to 7,000 acres of vineyards and then take the company public in two or three years as a REIT.

REITs are one of the largest players in California vineyard investments, with major holdings in Napa and Sonoma counties, either directly or as the financing behind such growth wineries as Kendall-Jackson. But a survey of REIT analysts indicates that while unloading vineyard assets may be good for Prudential, Beringer and other wineries, vineyards are a far more dicey investment, and much less suitable for REITs than traditional commercial properties.

WheatFirst REIT analyst Christoper Haley said that while he has a generally positive view of any continued securitization of real estate, a vineyard REIT carries with it many potential problems. "It does not have a significant investor base vs. timber or, say, auto dealerships." Haley added that there are no benchmarks for assessing its performance, making it "very difficult to price." Pointing to wine's relatively small U.S. consumer base, he said that a vineyard REIT "doesn't make as much sense as one for sod farms."

Jim Sullivan with Prudential Securities in New York agrees. "The fundamentals in the [wine] sector don't appear to be all that positive in terms of supply and demand." In addition, Sullivan pointed out that he felt there were other negative factors, including "limited possibilities for adaptive reuse"—alternative uses for the property.

Haley and Sullivan were part of our survey consensus that vineyards are far riskier propositions for REITs than commercial properties because: (1) they're not as profitable, (2) are subject to more sudden and uninsurable income losses, (3) are linked directly to consumer demand for a single product, which is itself a risky proposition, and (4) has limited alternative uses.

Vineyards are agriculture, and farming income has always been uncertain from year to year, depending on the weather, pests, and markets. The REIT advantage of generating tax-free income evaporates when the property fails to make money, as vineyards often do. Losing money also means a public REIT can't maintain the price of its stock, has less cash for operations, and can't attract the new investment capital needed for continued growth, and the stock price drops further, producing a power dive toward crash and burn.

Indeed, the record 1997 harvest—up more than 30 percent over 1996—and record prices for the grapes made vineyard REITs look promising in early 1998. However, the 1997 prices for grapes were artificially distorted by shortages that existed in the 1994 through 1996 harvests, prompting wineries to sign contracts for grapes at prices that were substantially higher than they would have been had anyone had any idea of the size of the harvest.

But there is a grape glut coming. Between 1993 and 1997, wine grape acreage in California soared from 326,700 to 403,800 acres, a 23 percent gain. Barry Bedwell, president of Allied Grape Growers, a cooperative of independents based in Fresno, said that by 2000 he expects acreage of such popular grapes as Merlot and Cabernet Sauvignon will increase by another 50 percent, with Chardonnay acres increasing about 40 percent, and Sauvignon Blanc and Zinfandel 25 and 22 percent respectively.

But there's more! More vineyards, that is. California's largest vendor of grapevines, Sonoma Grapevines, reported in July 1998 that they had sold more vines that year than ever before: 13.7 million vines—enough to plant about 19,000 acres of vineyards. This was a 24 percent increase over 1997. Significantly, the company reported that almost all the vines were for new vineyards rather than for replanting vineyards afflicted with Phylloxera.

Since Sonoma Grapevines has about 40 percent of the market, there are potentially 47,000 new acres of vineyards that will begin producing in 2001 alone. At a conservative five tons per acre and 142 gallons per ton, this means an additional 33 million gallons of wine coming to market that year. Bedwell said that most of these new plantings are speculative and do not have contracts to sell their grapes. "We're advising our members to go back to Economics 101 and not plant without a contract," he says.

The only bright spot is for grapes used in wines costing $25 per bottle and up, so-called ultrapremium wine. Demand, most agree, will be more in line with supply. But more than 83 percent of all wine sold in the United States costs less than $10 per bottle, and this is the price segment that is currently being hammered. Except for Chalone and LVMH, every public winery makes the lion's share of its revenues from wines costing less than $10.

Many in the industry were whistling past the graveyard, hoping that El Niño would cut the 1998 crop and that there would be an end to the imported bulk wine that California vintners used to fill their bottles a year earlier. But many of those contracts are multiyear and cannot be turned off like a faucet.

"It's a global market," said wine broker Karen Mancuso of San Francisco. "There's good wine going begging for $1 per liter. The price is soft if you can find a buyer." Mancuso and others pointed out that even if California wineries stopped buying imported bulk wine tomorrow, it would probably be bottled and turn up on store shelves anyway, exerting similar downward price pressures. If domestic wineries don't drop retail prices, then imports will continue to increase their market share.

In fact, the Central Valley grapes that are erroneously being dismissed as jug quality are now being turned into very good wine. Three of *Wine Spectator*'s thirteen best buys are made by Golden State Vintners from Central Valley grapes. Summerfield, GSV's own brand, costs $6 and under and has quality scores comparable to wines costing twice that much and more. Those will absolutely affect far more than just jug wine.

It's easy to see from this that even if wine consumption increased at the same modest single-digit rates it experienced in most of the 1990s, there will be an ocean of wine on the market, pushing down the prices of wine, which in turn pushes down the price paid for grapes and decreases vineyard profits. A renewed government push for alcohol controls and higher taxes, along with more vigorous neo-Prohibitionist campaigns, could drive down consumption as they have in the past.

In addition to wine consumption and grape supply issues, a vineyard owner, whether it be a farmer or a REIT, faces a daily struggle with pests that can devastate a vineyard or an entire region as Phylloxera did. Other pests such as Pierce's Disease, the newly discovered "Black Goo," Leaf Roll Virus, nematodes, and others could wipe out vineyard profits. While termites might pose some danger to a commercial building, careful maintenance minimizes the risk. More important, termites have a known cure, while the shoddy state of vineyard research leaves growers with more questions than answers when pests strike their vineyards.

Weather, too, can have an effect on commercial buildings, but the cash flow doesn't suffer when a season is cooler/wetter/drier than needed; rents don't go up or down with the weather. And a building tenant has no right to offer the owner less rent when the vacancy rate (office space supply) goes up.

Disasters are, of course, a different story from normal weather variations, but insurance coverage provides a wide margin of protection for commercial structures. Crop insurance is available, but is so expensive that it is far from universal for vineyard operators and owners.

Commercial real estate also enjoys more reliable financing from banks and other institutions, and is far less likely to have credit lines arbitrarily changed or dropped than vineyards and wineries. Commercial properties are also easier to sell because there are many more potential buyers. In addition, the owner of a commercial building can take a number of short-term actions to shape up a property for a good sale: new tenants can be brought in at reduced rents to increase the occupancy rates, and some maintenance can be deferred, both of which can beef up profits.

Vineyards, on the other hand, are long-term propositions. Trellising, the type of grape grown, yield, and quality, cannot be changed in one year or even two or three. If a varietal goes out of favor, or the demand is clobbered by imports or new vineyard production, there's not a damned thing the grower can do about it without a three-to-five-year process of replanting.

Commercial buildings are also far more versatile. Walls can be knocked out and rearranged; a light industrial park space can be converted to retail, to warehouse, to a health club or a church. If professional offices are not in demand, an office building can be filled with technology companies, toy makers, or any other type of business.

A vineyard, on the other hand, is a vineyard. Further, the premium vineyard properties held by Silverado and other potential REIT players are usually in areas with Draconian land-use restrictions that prohibit the land from being subdivided or used for anything other than agriculture. Whereas a light industrial park can be razed to build apartments or condos, vineyards in Napa and Sonoma counties are highly unlikely to receive permission to do anything other than grow something agricultural.

Commercial properties can also be built quickly if demand heats up. Vineyards, on the other hand, will not yield their first commercial crop for three to five years after planting. Further, if there is a huge demand for a particular type of grape, there may be a shortage of rootstock, which means a vineyard can't even be planted. So far, commercial construction has never been hampered by a shortage of concrete and steel.

Finally, a vineyard—like most agriculture—is labor intensive. Whereas commercial properties need minimal management and maintenance staffs, vineyards need people, a lot of people. And even the grunt workers in a vineyard need more specialized training than the commercial building custodian who pushes a broom. Vine pruning and other vineyard tasks, while not rocket science, still require training a lot of people in order for the agricultural maintenance and harvest to go right.

In short, vineyards are an extremely risky proposition in the best of times. They have numerous shortcomings that make them among the least suitable properties for a REIT. In the long run, vineyard REITs look as if they will not be profitable for the average investor and will primarily benefit only those people who cash out of their holdings by selling to a REIT.

Afterword:
How Things Could Be,
Might Have Been

Overall, this book's admonition to invest in wine and wineries "for the love not the money" presents a more sobering picture than the usual breathlessly optimistic assessments created by industry insiders and their cheerleaders: most trade publications and those who have already invested and want more company.

First of all, let me say that the conclusions here are not forever inevitable. If—BIG IF—the industry could promote itself, could cooperate, could abandon its snob approach and broaden its market base, could effectively fight back the neo-drys, could adequately fund research it desperately needs . . . IF it could do these things it has never managed before, then the financial outlook could reverse itself. Until then, a more realistic, cautious and less-than-optimistic approach makes a lot more sense than sheer optimism.

I started out with this blindly rosy outlook twice in my life, first when I founded my wine importing company, Wines West, in 1982, and again in 1991 when I started Wine Business Publications (since sold, and now among the industry's biggest cheerleaders).

So what cleared the scales from my eyes? Oddly, it wasn't the terrible difficulty of finding investors for Wines West, which I blamed on general economic factors. And the new clarity of vision did not come from covering the business side of the industry. I was so glad to have semi-retired from the hypersonic pace of Silicon Valley that I didn't think to compare wine industry financial returns and business practices to those of other industries.

No, what really made me sit up and take a look was the near-impossibility of finding investors to expand Wine Business Publications into the Web and consumer areas. This would have taken big bucks. So I went on a dance marathon, tapping, shuffling and jiving on the boardroom tables along Sand Hill Road in Silicon Valley's Menlo Park, the global epicenter of venture capital.

I knew a lot of the VCs from my days in technology. I'd been involved in tech start-ups and so thought this would be similar.

Wrong.

Everywhere I turned, in every VC boardroom, I heard an identical refrain: "The industry's too small; the tiny growth potential is not worth the risk; returns are too small; your market is shrinking."

Most business plans get tossed by the VCs; few actually result in invitations to present to the partners. The fact that we got through so many doors in person was testament that they liked the management team I had assembled and the financial performance of the business I had founded. In almost every case, I was invited, often encouraged, to contact them again if I had another idea . . . one that had the sort of growth prospects they could get excited about. They liked the talent; they liked the previous operating success; but as much as they liked to drink a really gnarly Cabernet, they just didn't like wine as an investment.

After each of these sessions, I'd go dig up more statistics to use in the next presentation, more facts, more stats that I thought would convince the next set of VCs.

But the response was always the same and after a while, I started to realize that these VCs were incredibly smart guys who had made billions for themselves and their investors. Could they ALL possibly be wrong?

I started seeing the wine industry through their cold, cruel spectacles. Some of them had netted in a year more than the combined profits of the entire wine industry during the same period. This is why early chapters of this book compare the wine industry's forgettable financial performance and prospects with other industries, especially technology, which produces more millionaires and billionaires in a year than the wine industry has collectively created in a century. In fact, if the *Forbes* magazine research on the richest 400 people in American is any indication, the wine industry has NEVER produced a billionaire. And it's damned unlikely, unless it changes mighty fast and mighty substantially.

I'd love to see that happen. I'd love to be wrong

because I love wine and despite all its flaws, I love the industry and the weird collection of ornery geniuses that populate it. Hugs and kisses, guys. Now get off your duffs and make something happen!

Appendix A:
Financial Ratios and
What They Mean

Debt-to-Equity Ratio and *Interest Coverage Ratio* are two key indicators of whether a company is carrying too much debt and whether it can service the debt it has. In addition to cutting investor returns, interest expenses from excessive debt can cripple a company by eating up working capital, reserves for a downturn, needed capital expenditures, expansions, and other vital expenditures.

In industries such as technology, which have substantial growth rates in the overall market, a company might wisely choose to borrow heavily, knowing it can earn its way out of the debt. But the relatively sad growth rates of the wine market, and the industry's inability to develop a coherent plan to increase growth, make it unlikely that a wine company can earn its way out of a heavy debt load. In addition, heavy debt is a time bomb because an increase in a half point or a point in interest rates could be sufficient to push a company to the wall.

Mike Kudy points out that the most profitable wineries in the Deloitte & Touche survey had a Debt-to-Equity Ratio of 2:1 or less. Mike Fisher at Motto, Kryla & Fisher said he thinks a winery is far better off with this ratio closer to 1:1 or less.

The Interest Coverage Ratio is a company's earnings (before interest and taxes) divided by the interest expense. This is a shorter-term measurement that indicates whether a company is generating enough cash to pay the interest on all its debts (short and long term). The higher this ratio is, the better. Fisher says that "the closer this ratio gets to 1:1, the more dangerous it is for the company."

A company with a high Debt-to-Equity Ratio and a low Interest Coverage Ratio is vulnerable and less likely to survive an increase in interest rates or a downturn in the wine market or general economic conditions.

WSRN's *QuickSource Fundamental Ratios Report* will automatically provide you with Debt-to-Equity Ratios and Interest Coverage Ratios.

Fixed vs. Current Asset Dollar Investments include the value of the company's property, plant and equipment, investments in joint ventures, and anything else not listed on the balance sheet as a current asset. To get this ratio, divide the value of these investments by the total assets of the company. The Deloitte & Touche survey found that the most profitable companies generally had less than 67 percent of their total assets in this category.

Wineries with a lower percentage in Fixed Asset

Dollar Investments are those that own fewer vineyards and will use contracted facilities for some of their wine production. While owning vineyards and processing facilities can provide for better control over raw materials and the vinting process, it also ties up a huge amount of capital that could be put to more profitable uses.

Current Asset Dollar Investments are cash and cash equivalents, accounts receivable, inventories, deferred income taxes, and similar assets. This percentage should be 33 percent or higher.

WSRN's *QuickSource Fundamental Ratios Report* will not automatically provide you with these percentages, so you will need to calculate them from a current balance sheet from a 10-Q or 10-K filing, which you can obtain from the company or one of the Edgar Online sites. If a Pink Sheet or OTC:BB company will not provide you with current financials, do not invest in that company (and tell all your friends about the experience).

Asset Turnover is a measurement of how hard the company makes its assets work for it and is calculated by dividing Annual Sales by Total Assets. The most profitable wineries in the Deloitte & Touche survey had a ratio of 1.0 or higher. Calculate from balance sheet and income statement.

Gross Margin measures the basic profitability of a company's products and is calculated by dividing Gross Profit by Gross Revenues. The most profitable wineries in the Deloitte & Touche survey had Gross Margins of 50 percent or higher. Calculate from income statement.

Selling Costs and *G&A* measure how efficient the company is at selling the product and at keeping costs down. This is calculated by dividing Selling Costs and

G&A (many income statements lump these together on the same line) by Gross Revenues.

The most profitable wineries in the Deloitte & Touche survey kept selling costs below 20 percent and G&A below 10 percent (30 percent for the combined). Calculate from income statement.

Profit Margin measures how profitable the company was overall and is calculated from the income statement by dividing Net Income by Gross Revenues. The most profitable wineries in the Deloitte & Touche survey had a Profit Margin of 18 percent or higher. WSRN will generate this number for you.

In addition to the ratios the D&T survey found revealing, there are four more (at least) that can help you assess the strength of a winery as an investment. These include: Return on Assets, Price/Earnings Ratio, Liquidity Ratio, and a new one we have created, the PERQ Rating.

Return on Assets measures how hard the company has made its assets work and is calculated from the income statement by dividing Net Income by Total Assets. This is calculated for you by WSRN.

Price/Earnings Ratio is a measure of whether a stock's per-share price is too high, too low, or just right, and is calculated by every online stock service on a daily basis by dividing the cost per share by the earnings per share (EPS). Most services calculate this from fully diluted EPS, which takes into account stock options and other deals which, if executed, would result in more shares being available on the market, thus diluting earnings. On the average, P/E Ratios of 15 to 25 generally represent the range of appropriately priced stocks, but this will vary somewhat from industry to industry. WSRN will calculate the P/E for you and also tell you how that ratio compares with other stocks in the same industry.

Be aware that stock prices are driven more by human irrationality than they are by the fundamentals of the underlying company, and only occasionally get connected to the economic reality of the balance sheet and income statement. Thus, a "casino complex" drives many stocks as investors bet on a dream instead of the reality. Company hype, journalistic euphoria over the latest, greatest thing, and the all-too-human desire to make a killing mean that equity markets resemble a high-stakes adult theme park with high G-force rides to fortune and ruin. As a result, some companies with losses or mediocre earnings will ride high, while those with more solid fundamentals (and the ability to ride out rough weather) become prom wallflowers which are underpriced. Look for these bargain stocks with solid underlying fundamentals and you are less likely to lose your shorts over the long haul.

Liquidity Ratio is a measure of how much dollar volume is required to move a stock's price up or down by one percentage point. WSRN calculates the ratio by accumulating the daily percentage changes of each issue's closing price for each trading day of the month. Absolute values are used, as only the magnitude of change is important and not the direction. Next, the total dollar volume for the month is divided by this total percentage figure.

LIQUIDITY RATIO = DOLLAR VOLUME/TOTAL % CHANGE

A high ratio indicates a stock that requires relatively heavy trading to move its price. A low liquidity ratio indicates a stock that moves on relatively light volume—either upward or downward. If a small amount of trading volume can move the stock up or down widely, then the stock is volatile and subject to the sort of roller coaster swings that can give the average investor vertigo or worse. These are the easiest stocks to manipulate, and because they are, they more often are jerked around by insiders and other dishonest operators. Despite their publicity efforts to convince you otherwise, the SEC catches stock manipulators about as often as the average speeder gets caught in radar: seldom.

WSRN calculates this ratio for you and makes it easier to choose companies with higher liquidity ratios.

A survey by Deloitte & Touche analyst Mike Rudy found that about 75 percent of the wineries in the United States were losing money in 1993. Improving economic conditions and the public relations spin from the serendipitous "60 Minutes" program on the French Paradox reversed that proportion, so that by 1996 more than 75 percent were making money. While the reversal is obviously good news, there is an important caution attached to it.

The caution: the wine industry, lacking coherent leadership or an aggressive plan to market its product, is almost entirely at the mercy of the general economic climate and of notoriously fickle consumer tastes. As a potential investor, you need always to keep firmly in sight that very *little* of the good financial performance by wineries in the last half of the 1990s was due to anything that companies, their management, or their industry associations did for themselves.

On the contrary, almost all of the growth can be attributed to two accidents: the "60 Minutes" French

Paradox program and a shortage of grapes from a com-
bination of weather and Phylloxera.

There are some notable exceptions, which you can
find by reading through annual reports and other statements. Remember that the record profits of wineries
since 1996 came about by raising prices rather than selling more product. While this can make the income
statement look good, it conceals fundamental weak-
nesses among those companies that have grown mostly
because of this. Because as they—and their investors—
are learning, record harvests like 1997, in the absence
of consumer growth, mean more bulk wine at less expensive prices, which will cause most wine prices to
fall.

For this reason, you should look past the income
statement and make sure that the winery you want to
invest in is showing substantial increases in volume
sales of wine as well as prices.

The *PERQ Rating* is a major one for people who
invest for the love of a company rather than the purely
financial gains it may bring them. Thus, many parents
buy Disney stock as a way to bet on a horse that runs
through their houses every day. There are also discounts on Disney merchandise, and other advantages
to owning the stock.

PERQs among public wineries include dinners,
trips, discounts on wine and other merchandise and
events. Because PERQs appeal to the senses and not
to the pocketbook, because they vary so widely from
company to company, and because they include special
occasions and events that are hard to evaluate in a simple dollar sense, you will need to assess these individu-
ally if the PERQs appeal to you. I have given each of

the public wineries a PERQ Rating from 1 to 10 (10 being best) to help guide you.

Finally, when speaking to your wallet instead of your heart, you need to decide whether an equity investment in winery stocks is really worth the risk to you. Mike Rudy points out that overall, the wine industry can produce a 15 percent return, involve considerable risk, and the returns are taxable. Tax free municipal bonds, on the other hand, involve little risk and were producing 7 percent returns in early 1998.

After taxes (assuming a 25 percent rate), this means the tax free, almost risk free muni investment is worth 8.75 percent after taxes, while the winery after-tax return is 11.25 percent. Is a 2.5 percent spread worth the risk? Is it worth the risk as a lifestyle investment? Is it worth the risk if you get wine discounts and nifty PERQs? You have to make the ultimate decision, but I believe that the financial analysis and Rudy's observations still point to my axiom that if you invest in wine, you're better off doing it for the love and not the money.

Appendix B

VINEYARD FINANCES *(all figures per-acre unless otherwise noted)*		(YEARLY)

GROSS INCOME:	$	7,726.50
EXPENSE		
$/ACRE (EQUITY IN PURCHASE)	$	340.00
$/ACRE (EQUITY IN CAPITALIZATION)	$	180.00
$/ACRE (OVERHEAD)	$	700.00
$/ACRE (FARMING COSTS)	$	1,500.00
$/ACRE (INTEREST)	$	2,912.00
$/ACRE (HARVEST)	$	562.50
FIRST 3 YRS LOST HARVEST INCOME		716.40
TOTAL EXPENSES	$	6,910.90
GROSS PROFIT BEFORE TAXES	$	815.60

ASSUMPTIONS		
TONS/ACRE	4.5	
$/TON	$1,717.00	
HARVEST COST PER TON	$125.00	
OVERHEAD	$700.00	
ASSUME NO PRINCIPAL PAYDOWN	INTEREST	
Percent Financed	70%	
Interest Rate	8%	
FARMING COSTS	1500	
COST OF LAND	$34,000.00	
COST OF CAPITALIZATION	$ 18,000.00	
AMORTIZATION PERIOD	30	
INCOME LOSS		
FOR LACK OF HARVEST		
FOR FIRST	3	YEARS
(MINUS HARVEST EXPENSE)	$ 7,164.00	

ANNUAL PRE-TAX % IRR (over life of vineyard, assume vineyard sale) =		6%

Initial investment	$	15,600.00	ASSUMPTIONS	
			%LAND APPRECIATION	60%
			INFLATION	2.5%
Equity in land & improvements	$	21,720.00		
Income over vineyard life	$	24,468.00		
TOTAL GROSS RETURN OVER VINEYARD LIFE	$	30,588.00		

This model assumes that the vineyard owner can finance the land and capitalization at the stated equity percentages and interest rate for the life of the vineyards and that the losses for the first three years can be financed with no interest, and further that there is no paydown of the principal of either the land or the capitalization. The original cost of the land and improvements pass through with the sale. Income and expenses are assumed to increase at the same rate.

Appendix 6:
The Coalition for Truth and Balance Statement

Wine and Heart Disease—
Behind the "French Paradox"

Numerous American and international research studies over the course of the last seventy years indicate that people who drink "moderate" amounts of alcohol on a regular basis have fewer heart attacks than people who either abuse alcohol or are nondrinkers. "Moderate" wine consumption is one to two drinks per day for men and one drink for women, depending on body weight. One "drink" of wine is five ounces.

In November of 1991, "60 Minutes" interviewed Dr. R. Curtis Ellison, chief of preventive medicine and epidemiology at Boston University School of Medicine, and explored the subject of the "French Paradox."

Americans, concerned about the intake of total calories, saturated fat and cholesterol, appear to have a greater risk of heart disease than the French, whose lifestyle includes a high calorie, high fat diet, more smoking, little exercise and an average annual wine consumption of 20 gallons per person per year compared to 2 gallons for Americans.

One explanation, Dr. Ellison noted, is that regular moderate consumption of wine with meals may make "it less likely for you to develop a thrombus, or clot, and have your coronary."

An early study of the relationship between alcohol intake and heart disease was conducted in Baltimore in the 1920s; the past two decades have seen many more. Numerous scientific studies find that moderate drinkers suffer fewer heart attacks—between 25 and 60 percent fewer—than nondrinkers. The protective effect of moderate alcohol consumption appears to be related to an increase in serum HDL (the "good" cholesterol), a decrease in serum LDL (the "bad" cholesterol) and inhibition of arterial blood clot formation.

Similar research results were found in Chicago and Albany, in Yugoslavia and Puerto Rico, in New Zealand, Framingham, and Massachusetts, among Japanese men living in Hawaii and Japanese physicians living in Japan, among West Australians and Trinidadians, among 276,802 men followed for twelve years by the American Cancer Society, among 87,526 women nurses and 51,529 male health professionals, and among 123,840 patients at the Kaiser Permanente medical centers in the San Francisco Bay Area.

Walter Willett, M.D., chairman, department of nutrition, Harvard School of Public Health, stated in *The New England Journal of Medicine* in January 1991, ". . . at present, the only dietary factor consistently associated with the risk of coronary heart disease in epidemiologic studies is alcohol, which apparently exerts [a] powerful protective effect . . ."

How can you reconcile health concerns with decisions about drinking wine or any other beverage containing alcohol?

The answer involves many factors, going well beyond the effect that moderate consumption of alcohol may have on the incidence of coronary heart disease.

Certain "at-risk" people should not drink any alcohol. This group includes alcoholics, people using drugs that interact adversely with alcohol, people allergic to constituents within alcoholic beverage products, people with other physical or psychological problems that make alcohol consumption unwise, and people about to engage in tasks requiring mental acuity or physical dexterity (such as driving or operating machinery). Other "at-risk" groups, pregnant women, nursing mothers and individuals with a family history of alcoholism should consult with their physicians about the health effects of drinking.

Nondrinkers should always check with their physicians to determine if they may be members of "at-risk" groups before making personal decisions about wine and alcoholic beverage consumption.

Scientific studies also indicate that the effects of alcohol consumption are "dose-related." Regular "moderate" consumption is where positive effects are observed. Binge drinking and heavy drinking may create serious problems (such as addiction, an increased risk of violent death, fetal alcohol syndrome and cirrhosis of the liver) that overwhelm any positive effect of moderate consumption on coronary heart disease. Scientific studies refer to this as the "U-Shaped Curve," where positive effects observed among moderate drinkers are diminished in populations of nondrinkers and alcohol abusers.

We believe that you are entitled to know the facts about wine and alcoholic beverages, both pro and con, so that you can make informed and responsible choices about consumption.

Acknowledgments

I want to express my gratitude to my long-time friend and editor at Avon Books, Tom Dupree, whose vision and hard work made this a far, far better book than the manuscript I first produced. Editing these days is a rarity in the book world, and good editors are far more precious than all the jewels in Harry Winston's display cases.

I am also infinitely grateful to Megan—my wife, friend and partner—whose love and support over the past eighteen years are so wonderful and steadfast that they transcend my ability to express them in words.

God has blessed me and I am thankful.